RAILWAYS
IN THE FORMATIVE YEARS
1851-95

Railways of the World in Colour

RAILWAYS

IN THE FORMATIVE YEARS
1851-1895

by
O. S. NOCK

Illustrated by
CLIFFORD and WENDY MEADWAY

LONDON
BLANDFORD PRESS

First published in 1973

© 1973 Blandford Press Ltd,
167 High Holborn, London WCiV 6PH

ISBN 0 7137 0612 0

Colour plates printed by De Ysel Press, Deventer, Holland
Printed and bound in Great Britain by Richard Clay (The Chaucer Press), Ltd,
Bungay, Suffolk

PREFACE

In filling in the gap between the period covered by two earlier volumes in this series, *The Dawn of World Railways 1800–1850*, and *Railways at the Turn of the Century 1895–1905*—the years 1851–1895—the artists and I have still been working on much pioneer ground. For the period covers the beginnings of railways in many overseas countries, including India, New Zealand, Japan and parts of Canada. Fortunately however the correspondence that has resulted from the earlier volumes has made many contacts for us in hitherto 'closed' areas, and with information now to hand we have been able to fill in a few of the more obvious gaps existing in our earlier books. This is particularly the case with Japan, through the kindness of Messrs. Y. Kawakami and H. Uematsu.

Again we have consulted many authoritative works, in many languages, and a list of these is given in a bibliography. Among individual friends who have given me much help I must mention Mr. R. F. Corley, of Peterborough, Ontario, Canada, Baron G. Vuillet, of Paris, and Dr. P. Ransome Wallis. My warmest thanks are due to them all.

Brock

Silver Cedars,
High Bannerdown,
Batheaston,
Bath.

July 1972

INTRODUCTION

By the middle of the nineteenth century railway development in the more advanced countries had progressed to the stage when the design of equipment and methods of operation had attained a marked degree of reliability; and although one could never describe the situation in Great Britain, France, Germany and the Low Countries as becoming stabilised, the innovations were becoming less frequent, as experience showed what was most to be trusted. In the vast tracts of scarcely developed country in North America, both north and south of the 49th Parallel, railroading was still in an exciting pioneering stage, with much of the practice still in an exploratory, but highly interesting state. Railways in the more distant and underdeveloped parts of the British Empire were in their infancy, while in India development was governed to a very considerable extent by strategic considerations. As was only to be expected British influence was strong in countries like Australia, New Zealand, the Cape of Good Hope and Natal but, somewhat understandably, less so in Canada.

Reviewing the locomotive position in rather more detail, in Great Britain the availability of almost unlimited quantities of good quality bituminous coal led to the establishment of a relatively small standard of locomotive power; the high quality of the coal made possible the use of small fireboxes, while the continuance of small four-wheeled and six-wheeled carriages, even on important long-distance passenger trains, kept train loads well below those becoming usual in North America and even in the developing colonies of the British Empire. On the Continent of Europe coal was available in ample quanti-

ties, but it was mostly of a quality far below that of the British coalfields, and in those countries which made a practice of using their indigenous fuel one saw, early in the period covered by this book, ingenious designs of locomotive to utilise lower grades of coal, and to ensure every economy in its use. This is not to say that contemporary British practice did not strive to secure efficiency in working; it was that Continental designers, faced with their particular problems, sought means of dealing with them that were then thought unconventional.

Concurrently, the development of passenger rolling stock was taking different forms. The relatively short runs in Great Britain, and the early commitment to individual carriage and wagon turntables in station areas, made the British development towards larger and more luxurious carriages relatively slow. But despite the longer journeys, and the far greater proportion of night travel, the general trend of development in Europe was slower even than in Great Britain. Some conditions of long distance night travel across Europe, even down to the turn of the century, were incredibly spartan, if not exactly insanitary! In North America two factors influenced a different trend altogether. The lightly laid tracks across virgin country, and the difficulty of maintaining a good 'top and line' in the extremes of temperature experienced led to the early abandonment of short, four-wheeled vehicles. The six-wheeler was hardly used at all. It was found that the bogie vehicle rode more easily on these early tracks, and it became the standard type from a very early stage in North American railway history.

The large bogie car, with a high

clerestory roof, was the almost universal form of passenger vehicle for well over 50 years. It was used not only for luxurious first-class travel but also for the lower order of passengers. In Canada they were termed 'Colonist' cars, and were used for day and night travel indiscriminately. The early passenger trains in the U.S.A. and Canada made a somewhat incongruous spectacle, with a train of these huge towering vehicles headed by a small 4-4-0 locomotive, garishly finished, and usually conspicuous with a large 'diamond' or 'balloon' stack. They made an extraordinary contrast to British and Continental trains of our period, the rolling stock of which consisted of small flat-roofed vehicles, above which the chimney and boiler mountings of the locomotives towered high.

The locomotives of Canada and the U.S.A. developed to suit the physical conditions of the tracks, the fuel available and the form of service established for train crews. North American coals were not suited to the British type of firebox. Much of that used was anthracite, which formed a large amount of clinker, and large grate areas became customary. Concurrently the tracking qualities had to be devised to suit the form of permanent way, and the relatively stiff, rigid wheelbase of the contemporary British 2-4-0 and 2-2-2 was quite unsuited to North America. The 4-4-0 became a very popular type, so much so that it became known, across the Atlantic Ocean, as the 'American' type. That the wheel arrangement also became very popular in Great Britain at a later period is irrelevant, for there was all the difference in the world between the bar-framed, outside-cylindered 'American', with a high-pitched boiler and a rather spidery appearance, and the later British

4-4-0 with inside cylinders, very neat and compact, with all the 'works' discreetly hidden behind deep valances and wheel splashers that covered nearly all the upper half of the driving wheels.

The structural restrictions imposed upon locomotive designers, in the size and weight that could be permitted, prevented the simple development of the thermodynamic features contributing to higher efficiency. One of the most important factors is the range of expansion of the steam. The greater the difference in pressure, between that at the moment of admission of steam to the cylinders and that at exhaust, the higher the thermal efficiency theoretically obtainable. But in a steam locomotive a certain amount of residual, or 'back' pressure is needed at exhaust in order to provide a draught through the blast-pipe and secure the rapid combustion of fuel that is necessary to maintain generation of steam. Two-stage, and even three-stage, expansion of the steam had been developed in marine engine practice, so as to spread the range of expansion over two cylinders, instead of one. This is the principle of 'compound' expansion, in which the steam passes through one cylinder, and instead of exhausting to atmosphere, is then routed to a second or low-pressure cylinder.

Compound locomotives in a great variety of forms were introduced on many European railways, including some in Great Britain; but during this period they did not immediately spread to North America. On the continent of Europe, however, the French and German developments were important and far-reaching. Some of the designs were possibly complicated to an excessive degree but in adopting the general principle of compounding certain British designers introduced systems of their own, which did not generally extend beyond the confines of their own railways. The principal difference between British and Continental compounds is that while the latter mounted the various valves, pipes, reservoirs and such like outside, till their locomotives were positively festooned with appurtenances, the British counterparts had all these basic necessities ingeniously concealed inside the traditional neat exterior. While the result might have been pleasing to the eye it often involved long and tortuous steam passages, which to some extent nullified any improvement in thermal efficiency that the compound principle provided.

As locomotives increased in size, and boilers increased in girth, a new problem began to arise, that of giving the driver a good look-out ahead. The length of boilers was putting the driver further back from the front of the locomotive, and while it still remained possible in many designs to provide a front window from which a view of the line ahead could be obtained over a shoulder of the boiler. this was tending to get more constrained. North American designers were at an advantage in this respect in that the loading gauge allowed for locomotives to be built taller, and the cabs at a higher level. So far as the cabs themselves were concerned there was always a striking difference between the amount of shelter provided for the enginemen on European and North American locomotives, the one being scanty, and the other elaborately enclosed from a very early date in railway history. The practice was largely traditional; for although winters in Canada and the U.S.A. are very severe, with temperatures of 80 and 90 deg. Fahrenheit below freezing point, it cannot be said that they are any worse than

some encountered in Scandinavian countries and in Eastern Europe.

The question of the look-out ahead naturally leads on to the question of signalling. The period of this book covers the vital stages in evolution of British signalling when block working was made compulsory on all passenger lines, and the lower quadrant semaphore became standard. There was, however, not yet a standard for the night indication of 'all right', or clear. Some railways had adopted green, while others were still using the old traditional white. The block signalling system, permitting only one train to be in a section at a time, was enforced by law after the terrible accident at Armagh, on the Great Northern Railway of Ireland in 1889. On the Continent of Europe a great diversity of signalling systems was built up, but it was only in Italy that the semaphore arm as used in British practice was used to the exclusion of all others. The Germans used an upper quadrant form of semaphore, while the French had a great variety of signs, chessboards, diamonds, discs and semaphores that could be most bewildering to an Englishman trying to understand them. One of the guiding principles of French railway signalling that an English railwayman found difficult to accept was that no signal at all signified 'all right': for example, the red and white chessboard meant 'stop' when displayed to the driver, but 'all right' when turned so that only its edge was visible.

In the meantime the North American railways, both in Canada and the U.S.A. had been perfecting the 'train order' system of traffic regulation. On many of the most important lines there were no signals, as such, at all. The driver of a train was given authority to proceed by a slip of paper, known as a 'clearance order' handed to him at the starting station. With this were often a number of 'orders' referring to various conditions along the line. Some of these concerned temporary speed restrictions to be observed at specific points, but the more vital, on single-line railways, concerned trains travelling in the opposite direction that he had to 'meet'. He would receive an 'order' to cross train No. 'XYZ', engine 'ABC', at station 'JKL'; and if he arrived at that crossing station first he would have to wait there until the other train arrived. Frequently, additional orders had to be given to trains en route, and our pictures include a view and description of a 'train order' signal, and its function. (Ref. 46.)

The word station conjures up a variety of impressions, from the cosy little English country station of the nineteenth century, with its smartly kept buildings, its flower beds and all its personnel taking a pride in its appearance; with the station master, porters and signalmen being well-known and highly respected local personalities. At the opposite extreme would be 'stations' out on the veldt in South Africa, where a train would stop to take up passengers apparently waiting in open country, miles from anywhere, to 'stations' on the prairies in Canada, where the most prominent feature of the vast extending landscape would be not the station building, nor yet the 'train order' signal mounted on it, but the group of huge grain elevators built along the siding parallel to the line and a landmark for miles in every direction. The large city stations got still larger. Some had to be completely reconstructed. But it was the little ones that became so typical of the period; and when it ended, near the end of the nineteenth century, there was no sign yet that little country stations all over the world would in not so many years begin to disappear.

With the rapid increase in the weight and speed of trains it was found that some of the structures of the earlier railways were inadequate to permit further increases, and notable improvements in construction had to be made. In North America a number of the highly picturesque timber trestle viaducts were replaced by steel constructions; in England a start was made in the replacing of Brunel's timber trestles by stone-arched viaducts, though these latter replacements were to some extent dictated by the need to widen the line to provide two tracks instead of the original single one. Another interesting widening undertaken in the early 1890s was that of Brunel's celebrated elliptical-arch bridge over the Thames, at Maidenhead, Berkshire. But one of the greatest feats in railway bridge construction anywhere in the world was the gigantic cantilever viaduct across the Firth of Forth, in Scotland, whereby the East coast main line to Aberdeen was shortened by some 20 miles. Another great bridge of this period was that carrying the north main line of the New South Wales Government Railway across the Hawkesbury River.

A new railway built towards the end of the period of this book, and having the utmost significance in the development of the British Empire, was the Canadian Pacific, completed in the late autumn of 1885. This great line, pictured in many of the colour plates, was in every way the economic, social and political lifeline of the recently established Dominion of Canada; and although it was constructed at a time when the British railway network was well established, and passing from its own formative years towards the era of railway pre-eminence in transport, much of the terrain across which the Canadian Pacific was carried was virtually unexplored, and involved the surveyors in the most incredible hardships—carrying on the work through the depths of the Canadian winter as well as through the sweltering heat of the prairie summer. As a constructional feat, the building of some 2,000 miles of line in less than five years ranks as one of the world's greatest railway epics.

During the period under review the value of railways in war time was vividly demonstrated in several parts of the world. Brief mention was made at the end of the previous volume of this series (*The Dawn of World Railways 1800–1850*) to the 'Great Locomotive Chase' during the American Civil War; but the Canadian Pacific was used to convey a considerable number of troops from the eastern provinces to Saskatchewan to assist in quelling the notorious Riel Rebellion in 1884. The line was not then finished; but by carrying troops from the east to the 'end of steel' on the north shore of Lake Superior, and

marching forward to where the next section of railway was available, the C.P.R. was able to transport a force of 3,300 men to Regina, Saskatchewan, in no more than ten days—a feat hitherto unheard of in Canada. In the South African War, just after the end of our period, the armoured train patrols formed an important part of the strategy of the British Army commander.

By the year 1895, although the systems in certain countries were only in course of construction and expansion, railways had spread—albeit no more than thinly in places—to every continent in the world and here, in the country of their origin, we had witnessed how speeds in excess of 60 m.p.h. could be maintained over a distance of more than 500 miles. The record run of the West Coast tourist train on the night of 22 August 1895, when the 540 miles from Euston to Aberdeen were covered in 512 minutes, was a fitting climax to the 'Formative Years'.

1 **Great Western Railway (England):** a 'Hawthorn' 2–4–0 passenger locomotive.

2 **Baltimore and Ohio Railroad:** a 'Hayes' ten-wheeler.

EUROPEAN PASSENGER ENGINES

PORTUGAL

3 **South Eastern Railway of Portugal:** the 2–2–2 *D. Luiz* of 1862.

NORWAY

4 **Norwegian Trunk Railway:** a 'Stephenson' 2–4–0 of 1861.

5 **Netherlands State Railways:** 2–4–0 locomotive No. 13
of 1864.

6 **Helsinki and Hameenlinna Railway (Finland):** a
British-built 4–4–0 of 1860.

7 **Midland Railway of Canada:** the *Adolph Hugel* locomotive of 1874.

8 **Great Western Railway of Canada:** the Stephenson-built 2–4–0 *Prospero*.

9 **Midland Railway of Canada:** an early 4–6–0 locomotive.

10 **Canadian Pacific Railway:** 2–8–0 mixed-traffic loco-motive.

THE AMERICAN SCENE

IOWA

11 **Wayside Station in Iowa:** Ackley, on the Illinois Central.

NORTH DAKOTA

12 **An American Timber-Trestle Viaduct:** Gassman Coulee, North Dakota.

13 **Transandine Railway, Chile:** bridge over 'Soldier's Leap' gorge.

14 **A Novel American Station Design:** the style of Henry Holly.

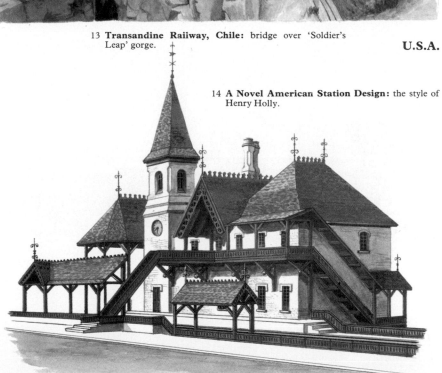

15 **Golden Spike Locomotive No. 1:** Union Pacific 4–4–0
No. 119.

16 **Golden Spike Locomotive No. 2:** the Central Pacific
4–4–0 *Jupiter*.

17 **Camden and Atlantic Railroad:** the *John Lucas* 2–4–4
tank locomotive of 1878.

18 **Denver and Rio-Grande Railroad:** a narrow-gauge
'Consolidation' of 1877.

CARRIAGES OF THE PERIOD

CANADA

U.S.A.

19 **Canadian Pacific Railway:** a 'Colonist' sleeping car.

20 **Denver and Rio-Grande Railway:** a four-wheeled passenger car.

21 **An Early Japanese Four-Wheeler.**

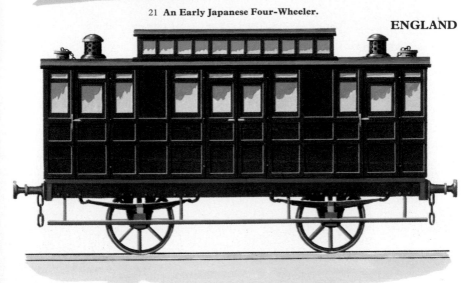

22 **London and South Western Railway:** a 'brake-third' of 1855.

EARLY TANK LOCOMOTIVES

NEW ZEALAND

23 **Otago Railways, New Zealand:** 0–6–0 tank engine of 1875.

NEW ZEALAND

24 **An Early New Zealand 'Fairlie':** the *Lady Mordaunt* of 1874.

25 **Festiniog Railway, North Wales:** the 'Double Fairlie' engine, *Little Wonder*.

26 **The First Locomotive in Japan:** a 'Vulcan' 2–4–0 tank of 1871.

27 **New South Wales Government Railways:** the '17' class
0–6–0 of 1865.

28 **New South Wales Government Railways:** the 'G'
class 2–4–0 passenger engine of 1865.

29 **New South Wales Government Railways:** the '60' class
0–6–0 of 1874.

30 **New South Wales Government Railways:** the '79' class
4–4–0 express passenger engine of 1877.

31 **Great Eastern Railway:** a rebuilt 'Sinclair' single.

32 **Great Northern Railway:** a 'Sturrock' 2–4–0 for mixed traffic.

33 **Great Western Railway:** a broad-gauge, 2–4–0 'Underground' tank engine.

34 **Stockton and Darlington Railway:** the 4–4–0 locomotive, *Brougham*, of 1860.

HOLLAND

35 **Netherlands State Railways:** 2–4–0 express locomotive of 1880.

FRANCE

36 **Northern Railway of France:** standard 0–6–0 goods locomotive.

37 **Holland Railway:** 2–4–0 locomotive built by A. Borsig of Berlin in 1880.

38 **Malines and Terneuzen Railway, Belgium:** a 2–4–0 passenger engine of 1872.

39 **Great Indian Peninsula Railway:** 2–4–0 locomotive for the first railway in India.

40 **East Indian Railway:** 2–2–2 express locomotive of 1862.

41 **North Western Railway, India:** 0–4–2 mixed-traffic
locomotive.

42 **North Western Railway, India:** 2–4–0 mail engine.

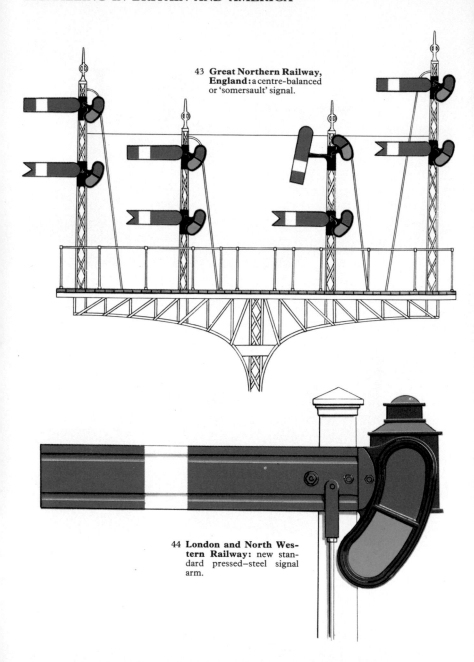

43 Great Northern Railway, England: a centre-balanced or 'somersault' signal.

44 London and North Western Railway: new standard pressed−steel signal arm.

45 An American Grade-Crossing: the highball signals protecting it.

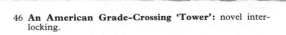

46 An American Grade-Crossing 'Tower': novel interlocking.

EVOLVING UNITED KINGDOM LOCOMOTIVES

ENGLAND

47 **Furness Railway:** a Sharp-Stewart 0–6–0 goods engine of 1866.

SCOTLAND

49 **Highland Railway (Scotland):** a 'Skye Bogie' 4–4–0.

48 **London Chatham and Dover Railway:** the 'Europa' class of 2–4–0 express passenger locomotive.

50 **Waterford, Limerick and Western Railway:** a 2–4–0 express passenger engine.

51 **The Westinghouse Brake:** the historic first test.

52 **The 'Last Spike':** the historic ceremonial completion of
the Canadian Pacific Railway.

STATICS AND STRUCTURES

U.S.A.

53 **Broad Street Station, Philadelphia:** Pennsylvania Railroad.

U.S.A.

54 **A Characteristic American Locomotive Shed:** the 'Roundhouse'.

55 **Chicago and North Western Railway:** bridge across the Wisconsin River at Merrimac.

56 **Paris, Lyons and Mediterranean Railway:** Monte Carlo station.

57 **Austrian Northern Railway:** 2–2–2 express passenger locomotive of 1873.

58 **Austrian Southern Railway:** 2–4–0 passenger locomotive of 1873.

59 **Austrian North-Western Railway:** 4–4–0 passenger locomotive of 1873.

60 **Austrian North-Western Railway:** 4–4–0 express passenger locomotive of 1874.

LATER VICTORIAN CLASSICS

ENGLAND

61 **Midland Railway, England:** a 'Kirtley' 0–6–0 goods
engine of 1868.

IRELAND

62 **Great Southern and Western Railway, Ireland:** 2–4–0
express passenger locomotive.

63 **Great Northern Railway, England:** a 'Stirling' eight-footer.

64 **Manchester, Sheffield and Lincolnshire Railway:** a 'Sacré' 4–4–0 of 1878.

GREAT STATIONS

GERMANY

ENGLAND

65 **The Anhalter Station. Berlin.**

66 **St. Pancras Station, London:** Midland Railway 1868.

67 **York Station:** North Eastern Railway of England.

68 **Worcester, Massachusetts:** the Union Station of 1877.

LOCOMOTIVE VARIETY

BRAZIL

69 **Sorocabana Railroad, Brazil:** a 2–8–0 freight locomotive of 1889.

SPAIN

70 **Andalusian Railways:** 0–6–0 goods engine of 1877.

71 **Swiss Central Railway:** 0–4–6 tank engine, *Genf*, of 1858.

72 **Madrid, Zaragoza and Alicante Railway:** an 0–8–0 goods engine of 1878.

73 **New South Wales Government Railways:** The Great
Zig-Zag.

74 **The Gotthard Line, Switzerland:** spiral tunnels near Giornico.

75 **Midland Railway, Settle and Carlisle Line:** Arten Gill Viaduct.

76 **The Forth Bridge, Scotland:** the towers under construction.

ROLLING STOCK—PASSENGER AND FREIGHT

GERMANY

77 **Baden Railways:** a passenger train brake van.

SWITZERLAND

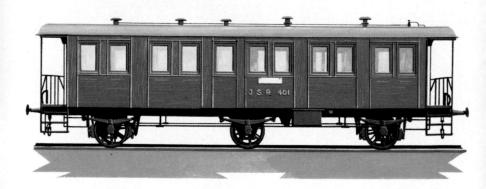

78 **Jura-Simplon Railway, Switzerland:** a six-wheeled
first- and second-class composite carriage.

79 **New South Wales Government Railways:** a passenger
carriage of the 1880s.

80 **Central Pacific Railway:** a typical freight train 'caboose'.

81 **Chicago Rock Island and Pacific:** the 'Silver' 4–4–0
locomotive, *America*.

82 **Delaware, Lackawanna and Western Railroad:** an
outstanding 'American'-type locomotive.

83 Louisville and Nashville Railroad: a 'ten-wheeler' of
1890.

84 Central Pacific Railroad: the *El Gobernado*, a 4–10–0
of 1883.

TANK ENGINE VARIETY

SCOTLAND

85 **Caledonian Railway:** 0–4–4 tank engine for the Cathcart Circle.

AUSTRALIA

86 **Victorian Railways:** 'E' class 2–4–2 suburban tank engine.

87 **Great Indian Peninsula Railway:** an 0–8–0 saddle-tank engine for Ghat Incline.

88 **Mexican Central Railway:** a Mason-Fairlie articulated 2–6–6 tank locomotive.

AUSTRIA

89 **Imperial Royal Austrian State Railways:** composite first- and second-class corridor carriage.

IRELAND

90 **Belfast and Northern Counties Railway:** first-class dining car.

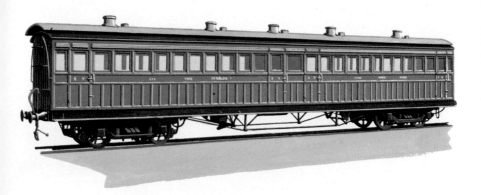

91 **Imperial Government Railway of Japan:** third-class
bogie carriage.

92 **Midland Railway of England:** a twelve-wheeled composite carriage of 1879.

DISTINCTIVE LOCOMOTIVES

U.S.A.

93 **Chicago, Burlington and Quincy Railroad:** a high-speed 'Columbia' type 2–4–2 of 1895.

ENGLAND

94 **Midland Railway, England:** a Johnson 'Spinner' 4–2–2 of 1896.

95 **Paris-Orleans Railway:** a 2–4–0 locomotive for light trains.

96 **Eastern Railway of France:** a famous 2–4–0 locomotive of 1878.

CARRIAGES LARGE AND SMALL

SCOTLAND

97 **North British Railway:** the first British sleeping car, 1873.

ENGLAND

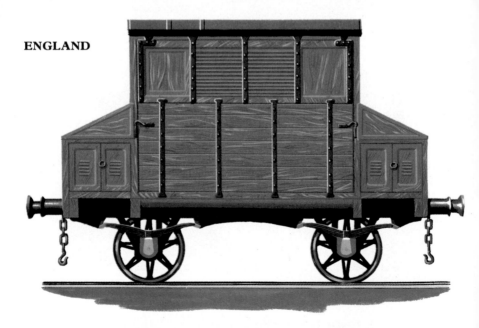

98 **Eastern Counties Railway, England:** a special horse box.

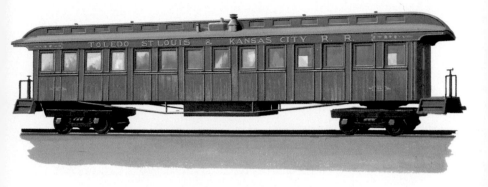

99 **Toledo, St. Louis and Kansas City Railroad:** a 'business car'.

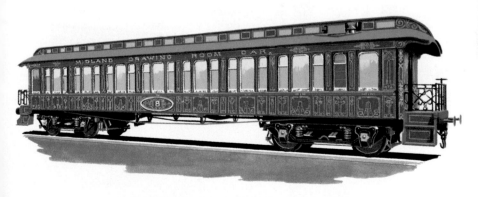

100 **The Pullman Car in England:** a Midland Railway drawing-room car.

COMPOUND LOCOMOTIVE GENEALOGY

ENGLAND

FRANCE

101 **Great Northern Railway, England:** Sturrock's master-piece, the '264' class.

102 **Northern Railway of France:** the 'Outrance' 4–4–0.

103 **London and North Western Railway:** a Webb 3-cylinder compound of 1885.

104 **Northern Railway of France:** the first 4-cylinder compound engine.

NOTABLE EUROPEAN LOCOMOTIVES

BELGIUM

105 **Belgian State Railways:** the 'Columbia', or type 12, 2–4–2 express locomotive.

FRANCE

106 **Paris, Lyons and Mediterranean Railway:** the first 2–4–2 express locomotives.

107 **Northern Railway of France:** De Glehn 4-cylinder
compound 4–4–0.

108 **The St. Gotthard Railway:** 4-cylinder compound
4–6–0 locomotive.

109 **Canadian Pacific Railway:** the first locomotive built by the company.

110 **Canadian Pacific Railway:** Stoney Creek Viaduct in the Selkirk Mountains.

111 **Canadian Pacific Railway:** entrance porch to the
earliest type of first-class sleeping car.

112 **London, Brighton and South Coast Railway:** the
'Gladstone' class 0–4–2.

113 **Great Eastern Railway, England:** the Holden 'T 19'
class of 2–4–0 express locomotive.

114 **Great Western Railway, England:** a 2–2–2 express
locomotive of the 'Sir Alexander' class.

115 **London and South Western Railway:** an 'Adams'
6 ft. 7 in. express locomotive, class 'T 3'.

116 **Victorian Railways:** the 'B' class 2–4–0 of 1862.

117 **Victorian Railways:** a first-class 'sitting' carriage of 1883.

118 **Victorian Railways:** the 'Old A' class 4–4–0 of 1884.

119 **Victorian Railways:** a Mann boudoir car.

120 **Imperial Government Railways of Japan:** a 4–4–0
used on the Emperor's train.

121 **Imperial Government Railways of Japan:** 4–4–0
express passenger-engine.

122 **Hakone Line, Japan:** an American-built 2–6–0 of 1897.

123 **Sanyo Railway of Japan:** an American-built 4–4–0 express passenger engine.

LARGER LOCOMOTIVE DESIGNS

INDIA

124 **Bengal, Nagpur Railway:** the 'A' class mixed-traffic
4–6–0 of 1888.

AUSTRALIA

125 **New South Wales Government Railways:** the '131'
class, 2–8–0 goods engine of 1879.

126 **New South Wales Government Railways:** the '205' class 2–6–0 of 1881.

127 **Imperial Government Railways of Japan:** 4–4–0 express passenger engine.

128 **Canadian Pacific Railway:** a colonist sleeping car.

129 **Canadian Pacific Railway:** interior of a first-class
carriage, 1895.

130 **New Zealand Government Railways:** the 'K' class
2–4–2 of 1877.

131 **New Zealand Government Railways:** the 'N' class
2–6–2 of 1885.

132 **New Zealand Government Railways:** a freight 'P' class 2–8–0 of 1887. .

133 **New Zealand Government Railways:** a 2–6–2 tank engine for steep-incline working.

134 **Philadelphia and Reading Railroad:** a 'Vauclain' compound 2–4–2.

135 **Texas and Pacific Railroad:** 0–6–0 shunting loco-motive.

136 **Chicago, Milwaukee and St. Paul:** an early 'Pacific' locomotive.

137 **Baltimore and Ohio Railroad:** 4–6–0 express passenger locomotive.

RACK RAILWAYS

U.S.A.

138 **Mount Washington Cog Railway:** the world's first rack
railway.

SWITZERLAND

139 **The Rigi Railway,
Switzerland:** the first
mountain railway in Europe.

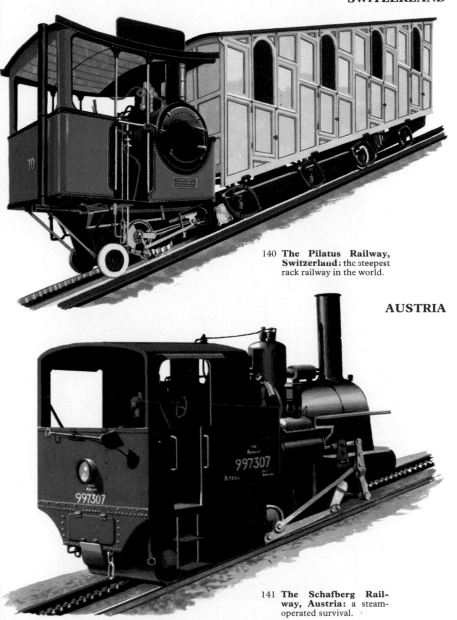

SWITZERLAND

AUSTRIA

140 **The Pilatus Railway, Switzerland**: the steepest rack railway in the world.

141 **The Schafberg Railway, Austria**: a steam-operated survival.

142 **New South Wales Government Railways**: the Hawkesbury River bridge.

143 **New South Wales Government Railways:** Albury
Station.

144 **Great Northern Railway:** the Stirling 8 ft. bogie single.

145 **North Eastern Railway:** W. Worsdell's 'M' class 4–4–0.

146 **North British Railway:** M. Holmes' 6 ft. 6 in. 4–4–0.

147 **London and North Western Railway:** F. W. Webb's
3-cylinder compound, 'Teutonic' class.

148 **London and North Western Railway:** the 2–4–0
'Precedent' class No. 790, *Hardwicke*.

149 **Caledonian Railway:** a 'Drummond' 6 ft. 6 in. 4–4–0.

TOWARDS THE TWENTIETH CENTURY

U.S.A.

150 **New York Central Railroad:** 4–4–0 locomotive No. 999.

SCOTLAND

151 **Caledonian Railway:** the second 'Dunalastair' class 4–4–0.

RAILWAYS

IN THE FORMATIVE YEARS

1851–95

1 Great Western Railway (England): A 'Hawthorn' 2–4–0 Passenger Locomotive.

At the beginning of the period covered by this book British locomotives were generally taking a more conventional and standard look, and this 2–4–0 can be considered a typical example. It was one of a series of eleven built by R. & W. Hawthorn for the one-time Oxford, Worcester and Wolverhampton Railway, afterwards known as the West Midland. It became part of the Great Western Railway in 1862, and it is in the livery of the latter company that the engine is shown. The structural design, with outside frames throughout, was one that was very popular at the time, and it has, indeed, been called 'Old English'. The engine can immediately be recognised as a Hawthorn product, because no other manufacturer used that highly distinctive shape of dome cover. Although of no more than moderate power by the standards of the day, with cylinders 16 in. diameter and 20 in. stroke, and coupled wheels 5 ft. 9 in. diameter, they were excellent engines, and had a life of nearly 50 years. Their last duties were on the Severn Valley line, between Worcester and Shrewsbury, which is now being preserved.

2 Baltimore and Ohio Railroad: A 'Hayes' Ten-Wheeler.

One could not find a greater contrast to the British 2–4–0 of the Great Western Railway than the seemingly fantastic 4–6–0 built for the Baltimore and Ohio in the U.S.A. in 1853. At that time Samuel J. Hayes was master mechanic of that railroad, and he was one of many American engineers who were becoming concerned that the length of locomotives was tending to interfere with the look-out ahead for the driver. Accordingly, he built the cab on top of the boiler. The decoration applied, even to the extent of framed landscapes on the panel sides, seems quite unbelievable; but quite apart from this the mechanical design of the engine was a very sound one, and was copied, with less fanciful embellishment, by other American builders. The Hayes engine is no figment of an artist's imagination. It is based on a coloured lithograph by Rosenthal of Philadelphia, and supported by a number of early photographs of engines of this type. It can be regarded as the progenitor of the 'Mother Hubbard type' of locomotive cab, which became very popular in the U.S.A. towards the end of the nineteenth century.

3 South Eastern Railway of Portugal: The 2–2–2 *D.Luiz* of 1862.

With Great Britain the pioneer in railway construction, it is not surprising that British manufacturers developed the craft of building locomotives and carriages more rapidly than those of other countries, and consequently were in a good position to develop the export trade in railway equipment. To a remarkable extent also, standard British designs were supplied. One could not find a more characteristic British express passenger locomotive than the *D.Luiz*, built by Beyer Peacock & Co. With outside frames for the leading and trailing wheels and inside frames for the drivers, it could be described as of the 'Jenny Lind' type, though the absence of a steam dome renders it very different in outward appearance from the typical 2–2–2s built by E. B. Wilson & Co. in Leeds. It was in service for more than 70 years and during that time underwent certain superficial modifications, such as the provision of a large 'balloon' stack to act as a spark arrestor when burning wood. The rail gauge is 5 ft. 6 in. This engine has now been restored to its original condition, and is preserved.

4 Norwegian Trunk Railway: A 'Stephenson' 2–4–0 of 1861.

At almost the same time as Beyer, Peacock & Co. were building the *D.Luiz* for Portugal, Robert Stephenson & Co. were supplying some extremely pretty little 2–4–0s with outside cylinders to the Norsk Hoved Jernbane (the Norwegian Trunk Railway). These were a typical Stephenson product of that period, though of very minute proportions to work in so mountainous a country as Norway. The cylinders were no more than 12 in. diameter by 20 in. stroke, and the coupled wheels 4 ft. 8½ in. diameter. There were only two of these engines, but they are of particular interest in that the second of them, named *Caroline*, has been preserved. This engine was sold to an industrial concern in 1919; but when the time came to celebrate the Norwegian railway centenary, in 1954, the little engine was bought back by the Norwegian State rail-

way, restored to its original condition and made fully operable. During the centenary celebrations it was in steam, and made a number of trips hauling a train of contemporary coaches.

5 Netherlands State Railways: 2–4–0 Locomotive No. 13 of 1864.

Messrs. Beyer, Peacock & Co. had a very long connection with Dutch State railways, and whereas some of the British manufacturers had the opportunity to supply only a few locomotives, which European countries subsequently copied, Beyer, Peacock were the principal suppliers to the State railway system for more than 50 years. No fewer than 33 engines of the type illustrated were put into service in the one year 1865, and others were supplied subsequently. They were splendidly reliable engines, having cylinders 16 in. diameter by 20 in. stroke, and coupled wheels 5 ft. 7 in. diameter. The illustration shows engine No. 13 as now preserved in the Railway Museum at Utrecht; but in their latter days all the engines of this class were fitted with cabs. As restored the engine has a highly 'British' appearance, and it was undoubtedly the influence of Beyer, Peacock that retained the very handsome, 'neat' look of Dutch locomotives for so long. This influence can be seen in the later design of 2–4–0, illustrated under reference 35 in this book.

6 Helsinki and Hameenlinna Railway (Finland): A British-built 4–4–0 of 1860.

To students of British locomotive practice a first sight of this delightful little engine will immediately suggest its strong likeness to the Highland 4–4–0s designed by David Jones. But then there is the fact that this was the very first steam locomotive to run in Finland, and that it was built in 1860 —*fourteen years* before Jones introduced his celebrated 'Duke' class. The likeness comes from the mounting of the outside cylinders on the outside frame, inclined, and with the crosshead guides fixed on the frame itself. Comparison should be made with the 'Skye bogie' (ref. 49). The arrangement of front-end framing was a speciality of Alexander Allan, and can be seen on the London & North Western Locomotive *Menai*, illustrated in *The Dawn of Railways 1800–1850*. Apart from the cab, which is in the American style, this pioneer Finnish locomotive is wholly British in appearance, not least in its ornate finish. Until 1865 the engines bore names only, like those of the Great Western broad-gauge stud in England. Numbers were added from 1865 onwards, and from 1868 naming was abandoned. The engine illustrated was the *Ilmarinen*, and the three sister engines imported from England in 1860 were *Lemminkainen*, *Suomi* and *Alutar*.

7 Midland Railway of Canada: The *Adolph Hugel* Locomotive of 1874.

Canada at one time had a Midland, as well as a Great Western Railway, though both, in relatively early days, were absorbed into the extensive Grand Trunk system. The amalgamated system as a whole operated in the eastern provinces and, serving Toronto and Montreal, was concerned primarily with traffic from the province of Quebec and Ontario into the U.S.A. rather than with the then undeveloped western regions of Canada itself. The Grand Trunk had an associated line, the Grand Trunk Western, by which it penetrated almost into Chicago on its own metals, and much of the seaborne trade in

which it participated passed through the American port of Portland, Maine. There was good reason for this because the natural trade route from the Canadian cities, down the St. Lawrence estuary, was completely icebound for many months of the year. Although the Grand Trunk and its constituents was strongly English in its management, American influences were strong in its engineering, and the locomotive illustrated will be recognised as based wholly upon American principles, and being in striking contrast to the early 2-4-0 shown under reference 8.

8 Great Western Railway of Canada: The Stephenson-built 2-4-0, *Prospero*.

The most uncharacteristic North American locomotive can be compared, most interestingly, to the *Adolph Hugel*. The 2-4-0 type was developed to suit British conditions. It is sometimes thought that the *quality* of North American permanent way, roughly laid, with flat-bottomed rails, was one of the principal causes of an uneven 'top', to use the civil engineers' term. It is, however, not generally realised to what extent the extreme variation in climate can affect the stability of the track, especially in the case of railways built to earlier standards. The variation, even between a cool night and a blistering hot day, can be intense, while the phenomenon of 'heave' in conditions of extreme frost can cause great trouble. The relatively rigid wheel base of the British-type 2-4-0 was soon found unsatisfactory, and the 4-4-0 became as familiar a feature of the Canadian railway scene as of that of the U.S.A. The various forms of spark-arresting chimney made a picturesque, if not very beautiful, addition to locomotives of the wood-burning period.

9 **Midland Railway of Canada:** An Early 4–6–0 Locomotive.

The development of the 4–4–0 into the 4–6–0 type in Canada can be studied from a comparison of this locomotive with the *Adolph Hugel*. The layout of the machinery is interesting in that neither of these two Canadian designs made use of the very short wheelbase bogie, which was originally derived from the use of a swing link attachment to the main frame, instead of the more conventional centre pivot used in later years. In other respects the Midland 4–6–0 is conventional, except in the absence of a sandbox on the boiler. The dome is over the firebox, as usual, and the safety valve carried on top of the dome. An interesting and important feature of this engine is the raising of the outer casing of the firebox well above the top line of the boiler proper. This provided additional steam space over the hottest part reducing any tendency to foaming, which would result in priming. In later North American design this feature was developed into the sharply-coned rear end of the boiler itself, which so impressed G. J. Churchward of the English Great Western Railway, and had so profound a subsequent influence on British practice.

10 **Canadian Pacific Railway:** 2–8–0 Mixed-Traffic Locomotive.

The completion of the Canadian Pacific Railway took place in 1886, with the driving of the last spike at Craigellachie, British Columbia (ref. 52). While much of the long line from Montreal through to Pacific tidewater, at Vancouver, lay over easy gradients on the prairie stretches, the line through the Rocky Mountains was exceptionally difficult and included some

gradients as steep as 1 in 25. On this section both passenger and freight trains were operated by small-wheeled 2–8–0 locomotives of the design illustrated. The passenger rolling stock was all of the large clerestoried-roofed type shown under ref. 19, and on the mountain sections the maximum that could be hauled by one locomotive was usually no more than two cars. To avoid putting an excessive strain on the drawbar of the leading car of a long train, multiple heading was not used in early days. The usual practice would be to have one locomotive at the head end, and then a second between the second and third car, and so on throughout the length of a train. By the time the C.P.R. was opened coal was the usual fuel, and the need for the special spark-arresting chimneys had ceased.

11 **Wayside Station in Iowa:** Ackley, on the Illinois Central.

The North American country station, particularly that of the nineteenth century, was a railway institution of immense character, quite unlike anything in the United Kingdom or in western Europe. Ackley is typical of the hey-day of steam railways in the open country lands to the west of the Great Lakes. There is a dwelling house, a shed, or 'depot' where all the passenger business was conducted and low buildings beyond which are the goods sheds. In between is a modest little example of a grain elevator. Today the grain elevators are about all that remains of many country stations in the prairie lands, but they are now of huge size, and half-a-dozen or more can be seen at one station. There is only one line of rails, and a large circular water tower for replenishing locomotive tender tanks. Prominent above the station buildings is the train order signal, with arms for both directions of traffic. The arm painted red facing the oncoming train is the one of which a driver must take heed, and in the position shown it signifies that there is an 'order' for him. There is also one for the next train coming in the opposite direction. These signals are further described under references 45–46.

12   An American Timber-Trestle Viaduct: Gassman Coulee, North Dakota.

It is axiomatic in any form of railway construction to use materials that are ready to hand, and in both the U.S.A. and Canada there were ample supplies of first class timber when the early railways were built. Furthermore there were many highly experienced craftsmen skilled in timber construction, and a large number of remarkable structures were erected spanning mountain ravines and broad deep valleys. The viaduct illustrated is an outstanding example 3 miles west of Minot on what was the St. Paul, Minneapolis and Manitoba Railway, when it was extended westwards towards the Pacific coast in competition with the recently completed Canadian Pacific Railway. This great viaduct, which was completed in 1887, is 1,609 ft. long, 102 ft. high and contains a total length of timber spars amounting to $1\frac{1}{4}$ *million* ft. Like the majority of timber viaducts, it was liable to damage by storm, flood or fire. It was breached by a severe gale in 1898, and replaced by a steel girder bridge in 1899.

13   Transandine Railway, Chile: Bridge over 'Soldiers Leap' Gorge.

The geographical situation of Chile, lying along a relatively narrow strip of country to the west of the great mountain barrier of the Andes, has led to many interesting railway locations, and some remarkable feats of engineering. While the main Chilean State Railway system runs north and south from Santiago, the capital city, a number of interesting lines were built into the mountain regions to the east, quite apart from the famous Antofagasta (Chile) and Bolivia Railway, which crossed the range, and entered the state of Bolivia. A short, though remarkable, line was built into the mountains from Los Andes on the metre gauge and extended for 55 miles through a truly fearsome terrain. The railhead was on a branch of the 1·6 metre gauge Chilean State system that linked with the main line from Santiago to Valparaiso at Las Vegas. On this metre gauge Transandine line was the highly spectacular section at the ravine known as 'Soldiers Leap', where the picture, more than hundreds of words of description, describes the kind of conditions faced by the engineers. This section was built by an English company.

14   A Novel American Station Design: The Style of Henry Holly.

While the city stations of the U.S.A. were beginning to show interesting and grandiose architectural treatment by the middle of the nineteenth century, the country station, as typified by Ackley (ref. 11) was plain, and purely functional. A distinguished American architect, Henry Holly, wrote a monumental book entitled *Country Seats*, which was published in New York in 1865, in which he stigmatised American stations as 'uninviting or ridiculous, beggarly or pretentious', and included in the book a design of his own, on which this illustration has been based. This took the form of an Italian-style villa; but it is interesting that it includes certain features to increase the safety of working. It related to a double-line railway, and the down and up lines are separated by a fence. To reach the lines on the far side of the fence one had to negotiate a series of galleries and footbridges, quite in the English style. One can imagine that American passengers, used to walking across tracks, would not take kindly to such precautions; but Holly's architectural style, and particularly the prominent campanile tower, was adopted in certain stations built subsequently.

15 Golden Spike Locomotive No. 1:
Union Pacific 4-4-0 No. 119.

In 1868 two American railways were pushing their construction forward to meet one another, and thus complete a continuous line of rails from coast to coast right across the country. One of these, forging westward, was the Union Pacific; the other, pressing east, was the Central Pacific. News of the progress of the friendly rivals was 'front page news' in the American newspapers: the Irish 'gang' of the Union Pacific, and the Chinese 'gang' of the Central Pacific. By the early months of 1869, despite severe winter weather, the 'race' went on, with the lines making their way, from east and west, round the northern shores of the Great Salt Lake in the State of Utah. Towards the end both sides were working almost night and day to try and lay the maximum mileage before the 'meet' and thus to derive the greater revenue from through traffic. The actual meet took place at Promontory, Utah, on 10 May 1869, when two 'American'-type 4-4-0 locomotives touched buffers, and a 'golden spike' was driven to complete the line. This illustration shows the Union

Pacific engine, the '119', built by Rogers Locomotive Works.

16 Golden Spike Locomotive No. 2:
The Central Pacific 4-4-0, *Jupiter*.

Apart from the smoke stacks, and variation in the gay colouring, there was little difference in basic design between the two locomotives that touched cowcatchers at the Golden Spike ceremony. *Jupiter* was built by the Schenectady Locomotive works, and both this concern and Rogers, who built the Union Pacific No. 119, later became part of the American Locomotive Company, 'ALCO'. The Central Pacific Railroad later became part of the Southern Pacific, and the link-up with the Union Pacific at Promontory completed the principal main line from Chicago to San Francisco. The portion of line on which the Golden Spike ceremony took place is now abandoned. The route was a circuitous one, with much severe grading, and in 1902-4 what is termed the Lucin Cut-off was built, crossing the Great Salt Lake, and saving nearly 44 miles on the journey. The present point of connection between the Southern Pacific and the Union Pacific is at Wells, Nevada, at the western end of the Lucin Cut-off line.

17 Camden and Atlantic Railroad:
The *John Lucas* 2-4-4 Tank Locomotive of 1878.

This unusual and pretty little tank engine was a 'one-off' job built by the Baldwin Locomotive Company to the specifications of Rufus Hill, master mechanic of the Camden and Atlantic Railroad. It was designed for a special duty, a shuttle service between Camden and Haddonfield, New Jersey. The length of run was only 6¾ miles, but the locomotive was in service night and day, and was scheduled to run eleven return trips every 24 hours. With turn-round mileage added, the locomotive covered 143 miles every day. To fulfil this schedule she was double-manned. She was the pride and joy of everyone concerned, and in her prime her running costs, including the wages of enginemen and cleaners, averaged no more than 15 cents a mile. After 12 years on this duty, she was sold to an iron-working firm, eventually found her way to Dutch Guiana, of all places, and was still in existence in 1927. The engine had cylinders 11 in. diameter by 18 in. stroke, coupled wheels 4 ft. 3 in. diameter and carried a boiler pressure of 125 lb. per sq. in. Her total weight in working order was $21\frac{1}{2}$ tons, and she ran, of course, on the standard 4 ft. $8\frac{1}{2}$ in. gauge.

18 Denver and Rio-Grande Railroad: A Narrow-Gauge 'Consolidation' of 1877.

The 'Rio-Grande' was wholly a line of the Colorado Rockies, and originally a 3 ft. gauge road throughout. It made an almost incredible way through fearful mountain defiles, on a track blasted out of the solid rock. Curves and gradients were tremendous. The 'Rio-Grande' was not alone in its intrepid penetration of the mountains. There were also the Colorado Midland, the Florence and Cripple Creek, and the Denver South Park and Pacific. Their locomotive power included 'Moguls', the inevitable 'American' 4–4–0s, and even a British-built 'Fairlie' presented to the Rio Grande by the Duke of Sutherland. In contrast to engines of this type used elsewhere (*see* refs. 24 and 25), it does not appear to have been very successful. The locomotive illustrated was one of the first

of the 2–8–0, or 'Consolidation', type used on the Rio-Grande. It was built by the Baldwin Locomotive Company, and was so successful that it became a standard class, with many subsequent additions. The cylinders were 15 in. diameter by 18 in. stroke, and the coupled wheels 3 ft. 6 in. diameter. Many of these engines bore names; the one illustrated is the *Silver Cliff*.

19 Canadian Pacific Railway: A 'Colonist' Sleeping Car.

It is no exaggeration to say that the entire development of Canada as a Dominion was bound up with the construction of the Canadian Pacific Railway. Immense national and personal resources in Canada were poured into the construction of the line; and when it was built and the trains were running, the development of the country itself took place first of all along the route of the railway. Emigrants from Europe landed at the Atlantic ports, or on the St. Lawrence. They were anxious to make their way west to the great open lands of the prairies, and they had long journeys to make by train. Even today the journey between Montreal and Winnipeg takes $1\frac{1}{2}$ days; it took much longer when the line was first opened and the emigrants or colonists had long nights to spend in the train. The sleeping accommodation was adequate if not luxurious. The interior is shown in ref. 128. The term 'Colonist' is still used today to describe some of the less luxurious, long-distance passenger cars, though not in any public literature.

20 Denver and Rio-Grande Railway: A Four-Wheeled Passenger Car.

In greatest contrast to the large bogie sleeping cars of the Canadian Pacific were the tiny little four-wheelers to be seen on the narrow-gauge lines in Colorado. These railways did not have to make long distance journeys, though the time taken was often far longer than scheduled because of natural hazards in the mountainous country. But small four-wheelers were not the most characteristic form of passenger car, even in those fastnesses. The typical north American bogie car, with high-clerestory roof, was equally in evidence, though these were not so tall in respect of the locomotives as on some of the standard-gauge lines. These little railways were built to the narrow gauge to economise in constructional costs, and this was achieved as much by reducing the height as the width. But for the legend on the side, this Rio-Grande four-wheeler could have belonged to one of the railways of the continent of Europe, in its primitive design and appointments.

21 An Early Japanese Four-Wheeler.

The early equipment of the Japanese railways was almost entirely British, and apart from the lettering, the small vehicle illustrated could have run on many an English railway in the latter part of the nineteenth century. There are five doors, but the partitions between the 'compartments' do not extend even as high as the windows. In this they were similar to the Great Eastern four-wheelers used on the London surburban services. This type of carriage was almost certainly built in England. A good deal of research among older and retired railwaymen in Japan has failed to trace the precise origin of many of the older vehicles; but later contracts were placed with the Metropolitan Railway Carriage and Wagon Company. A curious feature is the apparently 'double' roof, which was a characteristic of the

majority of early Japanese carriages. There was a central, very shallow, clerestory, and the roof of this portion was extended to the full width of the vehicle. This was used to provide some protection against the heat of the sun, and was a feature of early Australian carriages.

22 London and South Western Railway: A 'Brake-Third' of 1855.

In the spartan character of its design, there is not a great deal to choose between the Rio-Grande 'Smoker', the Japanese 'third' and this 'brake-third', for what was, by comparison, a thoroughly sophisticated English railway of mid-Victorian times. This had a central guard's compartment, with an enormous lantern roof, extending the full length of the guard's domain and acting both as a clerestory and a look-out post. There were two third-class compartments of the usual 'dog-box' proportions of that period, only 4 ft. 7 in. between the partitions. Even so, the third-class accommodation, though cramped, was at least covered in. At the same period the London and South Western Railway had a number of third-class 'carriages' with open sides— little better than cattle trucks! It is nevertheless remarkable to recall that vehicles such as that illustrated were still being built *new* in 1855, and without any form of brake other than what could be applied by hand by the guard.

23 Otago Railways, New Zealand: 0–6–0 Tank Engine of 1875.

Four locomotives of this design were built by the Hunslet Engine Company of Leeds for service on the 3 ft. 6 in. gauge line at the southernmost extent of the South Island, running from Winton, through Invercargill to the Bluff. They were built to the order of the Otago Provincial Council, but they did not stay long in the south. Being very strong and reliable machines they were transferred to Christchurch, there to work on both passenger and goods trains. A factor that contributed to their early success was their relatively high weight for a small, 3 ft. 6 in. gauge tank engine of 27¾ tons. As originally supplied, they had large wooden cowcatchers at the chimney end only. It is presumed that facilities were available for turning them, and that there was no need to run bunker first. When they were transferred from Invercargill to Christchurch—which transference had to be made by sea!—the cowcatchers were removed. After some 15 years' service it was found necessary to rebuild them in such a form as to reduce the maximum axle load, and enable them to run on lighter tracks. They were altered to the 2-4-4 wheel arrangement, and in this form they survived until 1925-8.

24 An Early New Zealand 'Fairlie': The *Lady Mordaunt* of 1874.

It is perhaps appropriate to place this pretty New Zealand Fairlie adjacent in this book to the 'father' of all 'double Fairlies', the *Little Wonder* of the Festiniog Railway. The *Lady Mordaunt* was one of two identical engines built by the Avonside Engine Company of Bristol, the second of which went to the North Island, to work in the Auckland district. The *Lady Mordaunt*, shipped in parts, went to Dunedin for erection. From there she had a somewhat unconventional trial run. The superintendent ordered a stop alongside the local brewery, and called for a christening there and then. One would then imagine that the christening was carried out with

beer rather than champagne! As a locomotive she was not only interesting as an example of the Fairlie type, but as the very first British-built locomotive to have the Walschaerts valve gear. Apparently she did not have the same success as her Welsh counterparts, being regarded as a poor engine with any load. She was scrapped in 1896, but one of the bogies of her sister engine was preserved, and in due course was transferred to the Science Museum in London.

25 Festiniog Railway, North Wales: The 'Double Fairlie' Engine, *Little Wonder*.

This incredible little engine was built and tested on the Festiniog Railway in 1869. She ran on the 1 ft. 11½ in. gauge and was much smaller and lighter than the New Zealand *Lady Mordaunt*. Her cylinders were 8¼ in. diameter by 13 in. stroke, against 9 in. by 16 in. The main advantage of the Welsh engine was that she carried a pressure of 160 lb. per sq. in. against 130 lb. But on the steep gradients and incessant curvature of the Festiniog Railway she would seemingly take almost any load. On special test occasions she hauled trains of more than 200 tons. She was an immense success, and more Fairlie engines were added to the stock. One observer, after certain up-grade tests, remarked that he would be quite prepared to work the traffic of the London and North Western Railway with such engines! The Festiniog performance started a new vogue for *very* narrow-gauge railways in many parts of the world, as well as showing the merits of articulated locomotives on curved stretches of line. Two locomotives of the Fairlie type, developed from the original *Little Wonder*, are still in service on the Festiniog Railway today.

26 The First Locomotive in Japan: A 'Vulcan' 2–4–0 Tank of 1871.

This neat little engine was one of a small group that inaugurated the railway era in Japan. It has now been preserved and is housed in the Japanese railway museum. There it is painted dark green, but historians cannot trace any reason for this colour having been used. The brown livery, with black boiler shown in this illustration, is based on a series of contemporary, Japanese-coloured prints which, although crudely drawn and coloured, show a style of painting that corresponds exactly with the builders' photograph of the engine. One of these prints is strongly reminiscent of early views on the English Stockton and Darlington Railway, with horse-drawn vehicles racing the train. The Japanese drawing, with much local colour, includes one-manpower rickshaws also racing the train! Nevertheless photographs show locomotives of this class hauling 12 four-wheeled coaches. Later engines of the same general type had copper-capped chimneys, and carried the number in brass numerals on the chimney front.

27 New South Wales Government Railways: The '17' Class 0–6–0 of 1865.

The gradual extension of the main line south from Sydney and the existence of some sections of severe grading made it necessary to have goods engines of greater power. Although the length of run was likely to be much longer, there was some similarity in working conditions to those on the Stockton and Darlington Railway, and a contract was placed with Robert Stephenson & Co. for 15 locomotives of the 0–6–0 'long-boilered' type. The origin of this is described in a previous volume in

this series, *The Dawn of World Railways 1800–1850.* It consisted essentially in having a long boiler barrel, to suppress as far as possible the emission of sparks, and a relatively small firebox. It was ideal for a goods engine on intermittent duty, because the long boiler provided a reservoir for building up, and maintaining, a good head of steam, while the small firebox reduced the stand-by losses, by having a lesser amount of coal burning. There were, altogether, 23 of these Australian 0–6–0s, a further 8 being subsequently added to the original 15. They had 18 in. by 24 in. cylinders, 4 ft. diameter coupled wheels, and a boiler pressure of 120 lb. per sq. in. They were hard-worked and long-lived engines; the last of them was not taken out of service until 1953 when it was 98 years old! It is now preserved in the railway museum at Enfield.

28 New South Wales Government Railways: The 'G' Class 2–4–0 Passenger Engine of 1865.

While Robert Stephenson & Co. were providing 0–6–0 goods engines for this rapidly-growing State railway system, a contract for some of the earliest passenger engines went to the equally famous English firm of Beyer, Peacock & Co. of Manchester. These handsome little 2–4–0s were the first of a long succession of locomotives supplied to New South Wales by this firm. The 'G', or '23' class was very similar in general outward appearance to the 2–4–0 tank engines supplied to various narrow-gauge railways, of which the Isle of Man, and the Ballymena and Larne, in Northern Ireland, may be mentioned. The upward slope of the running plate, to clear the inclined outside cylinders was typical, while the bell-topped dome, and shape of chimney, were equally typical of Beyer, Peacock. The large canopy over the footplate was of course an Australian requirement to provide shade from the fierce sun of midsummer. The cylinders were 18 in. by 24 in., and in the first batch of three engines the coupled wheels were 5 ft. 9 in. In later batches the diameter was reduced to 5 ft. 6 in. to give higher tractive effort. At a later date weights were added to the footplate of some of these engines to provide extra adhesion. The boiler pressure, as usual then in New South Wales, was 120 lb. per sq. in.

29 New South Wales Government Railways: The '60' Class 0–6–0 of 1874.

The exceptionally severe gradients of the Western line, where it crosses the Blue Mountains, called for increased locomotive power, both for passenger and goods service, and the N.S.W.G.R. turned to the Stephenson 'long-boilered' type once again for *passenger* service. The relatively short wheel-base made the type suitable for working over the succession of sharp curves, while the constant stopping and starting, in working over the zig-zag locations, made the long boiler and small firebox ideal. These engines had cylinders exceptionally large for the period—19 in. diameter by 28 in. stroke—and enabled vigorous starts to be made on the heavy gradients. Except for the canopied cab the had a strong flavour of north-eastern England, in the Fletcher era, with the austere stove-pipe chimney, sloping smokebox door, and typically English headlamps. There were 6 of these engines constructed by Robert Stephenson & Co., but shipped in parts and erected on arrival in Sydney by Mort & Co. They worked passenger trains on the Blue Mountains

route for 10 years, and were then superseded by some American-built 2–6–0s.

30 New South Wales Government Railways: The '79' Class 4–4–0 Express Passenger Engine of 1877.

This was destined to become one of the most famous of all nineteenth century Australian locomotive classes. It was a direct development of the 'G' or '23' class (ref. 28) but fitted with a four-wheeled Bissell truck instead of the two-wheeled pony truck of the 2–4–0s. The four-wheeled 'truck' was not a bogie in the generally accepted sense, in that it did not have a central pivot, but moved instead on a radial arm, pivoted from a point a little ahead of the leading pair of coupled wheels. It was because of this that the wheels of the Bissell truck had to be placed close together. But 'trucks' apart, the '79' class were splendid engines. They were designed by Beyer, Peacock & Co., and that firm built the first 30. The Glasgow form of Dübs & Co. built 26 more in 1880–1, and further engines were added bringing the total strength of the class up to 68. They had long and strenuous lives, and no fewer than three of them are preserved. One stands on a plinth outside Canberra station; a second is in full working order, and used on 'Vintage' trains, while the third is to be exhibited in the Museum of Applied Arts and Sciences in Sydney. They had 18 in. by 24 in. cylinders, 5 ft. 6 in. diameter coupled wheels, and carried a boiler pressure of 140 lb. per sq. in.

31 Great Eastern Railway: A Rebuilt 'Sinclair' Single.

For many years in the mid-Victorian era the mainstay of the passenger service in

East Anglia was a class of 2-2-2 'single-wheelers' designed by Robert Sinclair, with 7 ft.-diameter driving wheels. As originally built, they were picturesque, but 'functional' looking engines, with a high, though attenuated cab, stove-pipe chimneys and a generally 'stumpy' appearance. They were nevertheless good engines in traffic, though the speed of service and the loads of the trains were not very demanding. Then S. W. Johnson was appointed locomotive superintendent; he was a veritable artist among locomotion engineers, and during his short stay on the Great Eastern, before moving to the Midland Railway, he rebuilt two of the Sinclair singles into the exquisite little 'period-pieces' shown in this illustration. He temporarily discarded the traditional blue livery of the Great Eastern for the 'yellow' of the London, Brighton and South Coast, put on the graceful boiler mountings that became characteristic of all his engines on the Midland and substituted a leading bogie. All that remained externally of the old 'Sinclair's' were the high, inclined, outside cylinders, and the double-tiered slotted splashers. The engine illustrated, No. 291, worked for many years from Kings Lynn, until she was scrapped in 1893 after 30 years' service.

32 Great Northern Railway: A 'Sturrock' 2-4-0 for Mixed Traffic.

Archibald Sturrock was for a time one of the foremost locomotive engineers in Great Britain, constantly striving to produce larger and more powerful locomotives, and to promote, if he could, the scheduling of faster trains. How his very large 2-4-0 express locomotives influenced contemporary French practice is described under references 101-104. But express passenger trains, and particularly those needing locomotives of maximum power, were few and far between in mid-Victorian days, and the Great Northern Railway needed many locomotives of intermediate power that could haul light passenger, and fast goods, trains. Sturrock produced a 2-4-0 design with 6 ft. coupled wheels for such a duty, and the illustration shows one of these, running at a somewhat later date, after having been reboilered by Sturrock's successor, Patrick Stirling. It retains all the characteristics of Sturrock's machinery design, with outside frames, but has the Stirling cut-away cab, 'straightback' boiler, and handsome, brass, safety-valve mounting. This engine was a familiar sight for many years on local trains between London and Hitchin.

33 Great Western Railway: A Broad-gauge, 2-4-0 'Underground' Tank Engine.

To gain direct access to the City of London, the Great Western Railway assisted in sponsoring the construction of the Metropolitan Railway between Paddington and Farringdon Street, the first 'Underground' railway in the world, which was opened in 1863. The Underground tunnels were made large enough to take broad-gauge trains on the 7 ft. gauge, so that Great Western trains could work through; but a difficulty arose in that the Act of Parliament authorising the construction of the railway compelled the use of locomotives that consumed their own steam and smoke. Daniel Gooch, the ever-famous locomotive engineer of broad-gauge days, designed a special class of 2-4-0 tank engines, with outside cylinders specially for Underground service. They were equipped with a device that enabled the driver to turn the exhaust into condensing tanks, instead of discharging it from the chimneys. They were squat, curious-looking engines—all the more so when seen from the front; and then their extreme width to suit the 7 ft. rail gauge became apparent. They did not remain long on the Underground passenger service because, following a dispute between the two companies, this was temporarily taken over by the Great Northern until the Metropolitan Railway had locomotives of its own.

34 Stockton and Darlington Railway: The 4-4-0 Locomotive, *Brougham*, of 1860.

When one refers to the Stockton and Darlington Railway, the mind naturally turns to the very earliest days of world railways; but actually this pioneer railway remained an independent concern until 1863. It had an interesting westerly off-shoot, known as the South Durham and Lancashire Union, which extended across the Pennines to make a junction with the London and North Western at Tebay. For this line, Thomas Bouch built two remarkable 4-4-0 locomotives, the *Brougham* and the *Lowther*. Technically, they were outstanding in being the very first bogie, four-coupled engines ever to run in Great Britain. They were not large locomotives in themselves, but the most striking external feature was the enormous closed-in cab, savouring more of North American than of British practice. But the humanitarian intentions of their designer, in providing his men with protection against the weather on that wild, exposed stretch of railway, were not appreciated. From all accounts the drivers and firemen disliked being closed in, and all subsequent engines, for many years afterwards, had the scantiest of weatherboards—no cabs at all!

None of these early 4-4-0s lasted long in their original condition. A sturdy, straightforward 2-4-0 was much more suitable for that railway.

35 Netherlands State Railways: 2-4-0 Express Locomotive of 1880.

The close collaboration between Beyer, Peacock & Co. and the State Railway resulted, in 1880, in one of the most beautiful and successful locomotives ever exported from England in the nineteenth century. No fewer than 176 of them were purchased. They were powerful, as well as fast, and were used on freight as well as passenger trains. Despite the use of large headlamps, they were essentially British in design. Although the earlier 2-4-0s supplied by Beyer, Peacock & Co. (ref. 5) had the Allan straight-link motion these larger engines had the Stephenson link motion. Their proportions were large, with cylinders 18 in. diameter by 26 in. stroke; the coupled-wheels were 7 ft. in diameter, and the boiler pressure 150 lb. per sq. in. Their elegant appearance made a strong contrast to that of the contemporary 2-4-0s of the Holland Railway (ref. 37) which can be well appreciated from a study of examples of both designs in the Dutch Railway Museum at Utrecht.

36 Northern Railway of France: Standard 0-6-0 Goods Locomotive.

This design was the freight equivalent of the 'Outrance' express passenger 4-4-0, and shows clearly the strong English influence that existed in Nord locomotive design in the seventies and eighties of last century. A total of 112 of these locomotives was put into service between 1883 and 1891, and all were built by the

Société Alsacienne, of Belfort. It is, however, not always appreciated that the famous chief engineer of that firm, Alfred de Glehn, was an Englishman, yet one whose entire professional life was spent in France. The Nord 0–6–0s were 'English' in having inside cylinders, Stephenson link motion and outside frames; but they were 'French' in the appliances mounted on top of the boiler, and in the curious little four-wheeled tender. Like the 'Outrance' 4–4–0s they were massively built, and their basic dimensions made them ideal for mixed-traffic duties. They had cylinders 19 in. diameter by 24 in. stroke; coupled wheels 5 ft. 6 in. diameter, and carried a boiler pressure of 145 lb. per sq. in. One of these locomotives has been saved from the scrap-heap and will be preserved in the railway museum at Mulhouse.

37 Holland Railway: 2–4–0 Locomotive built by A. Borsig of Berlin in 1880.

The locomotive described under reference 35 belonged to the State Railway of the Netherlands, but a stranger appreciating that title might be surprised to find that a second railway was operating in the same country. In fact there were *four* others! The State Railway ran from the packet station of Flushing to the German frontier at Venlo; the Holland Railway went north from Rotterdam through The Hague to Amsterdam; then there was the Netherlands Central running from Utrecht to Zwolle, the Netherlands Rhenish Railway, which the travellers from England encountered immediately on landing at the Hook of Holland, and finally there was the North Brabant. *Nestor*, the Holland Railway 2–4–0 illustrated, is a typical Borsig product: quite plain and functional, with a large wooden cab designed to minimise

noise. She was a locomotive of considerably less power than the British-built 2–4–0 for the State Railway, having cylinders 16 in. diameter by 22 in. stroke. The coupled wheels were 6 ft. 1 in. diameter, and the boiler pressure 150 lb. per sq. in. A total of 29 was built between 1878 and 1883, and the one preserved at Utrecht dates from 1880.

38 Malines and Terneuzen Railway, Belgium: 2–4–0 Passenger Engine of 1872.

This handsome engine, built by Beyer, Peacock & Co., could in some respects be regarded as the prototype of the Dutch 2–4–0 (ref. 35), particularly in regard to the boiler. It was in fact the very first instance of a Belpaire firebox being constructed in Great Britain. Alfred Jules Belpaire was himself a Belgian, having been born at Ostend in September 1820. Apart from the form of firebox that bears his name his work brought him International honours from France, Holland, Spain and Russia, in addition to his native Belgium. The merit of the square-topped firebox is that it facilitates the staying between the outer casing and the firebox proper. This Belgian 2–4–0 has the characteristic Beyer chimney and dome cover, and a very presentable cab for that era, but is of generally smaller proportions than the Dutch engine, reference 35. In view of the wide, subsequent application of the Belpaire firebox on so very many British, and British-exported, locomotives this first application is of historic interest.

39 Great Indian Peninsula Railway: 2–4–0 Locomotive for the First Railway in India.

Railways in India were planned in the first place purely on a strategic basis, and while the 5 ft. 6 in. gauge was chosen for principal main routes, a system of feeder lines on the metre gauge was considered, while still lighter railways on a narrower gauge yet were contemplated. The first railway to be opened for traffic was that between Bombay and Thana, which became part of the Great Indian Peninsula system. Naturally nothing but British equipment was at first ordered, and the locomotives for this line were built by the Vulcan Foundry Ltd, in 1851. They were of the simplest style of construction with inside frames throughout, and the old fashioned 'haystack' type of boiler. Dimensionally they were very small, with cylinders only 13 in. diameter by 20 in. stroke, and coupled wheels 5 ft. in diameter. But they were adequate for the earliest days, when the line was opened on 16 April 1853. It was no more than a modest start to what became one of the great railways of the world, in traffic and status as well as in name.

40 **East Indian Railway:** 2–2–2 Express Locomotive of 1862.

Just as the Great Indian Peninsula Railway originated in Bombay, so the East Indian began in Calcutta, and began to create the important trunk line that extended westward up the valley of the Ganges. The mail trains from the earliest days were of paramount importance, and ten pretty little 2–2–2 singles were built specially for this service. Unlike the pioneer locomotives on the G.I.P.R. these East Indian singles were from the outset provided with large canopies over the cabs. The mail drivers in those early days were all Europeans and they had to be protected from the heat and glare of the Indian sunshine. The locomotives themselves were of very simple

design, somewhat resembling, in the spacing of their wheelbase, the 'Lady of the Lake' class on the London and North Western, but with a running plate that was straight throughout. They had cylinders 15 in. diameter by 22 in. stroke, and driving wheels 6 ft. 6 in. diameter. The firebox was relatively large for that period, having a grate area of 18 sq. ft. The tenders were also large, and had a water capacity of 1,400 gallons.

41 **North Western Railway, India:** 0–4–2 Mixed-Traffic Locomotive.

The North Western Railway of India, a State-owned system, was formed by the purchase, by the State, of the one-time Scinde, Punjab and Delhi Railway, and its amalgamation with three smaller State-owned lines to the north of Delhi. The Scinde railway, opened for traffic in 1859 over two small sections, but it was opened throughout from Karachi to Kotri in 1861. One of the most important early classes of locomotive was the 0–4–2 mixed traffic, later classified 'KS' in North Western Railway stock, and here shown in the N.W.R. livery. This class is of particular interest in that one example, the *Eagle*, has been preserved. There is considerable doubt, even among the most erudite of researchers, as to what the livery of the Scinde, Punjab and Delhi Railway was. When she was first put on exhibition outside the locomotive shops at Moghalpura, in 1928, she was painted black, and lined in the style of the English L.N.W.R. Later, however, when she was exhibited in Lahore and in Delhi she was finished in full English G.W.R. style. We have preferred to show one of these engines in the normal working style of the N.W.R. These engines had 17 in. by 24 in. cylinders, coupled wheels 5 ft. 6 in. diameter, and a boiler pressure of 140 lb. per sq. in.

42 North Western Railway, India: 2–4–0 Mail Engine.

As on other Indian railways, mail trains on the North Western were given the highest priority, and the handsome 2–4–0 illustrated belonged to the class responsible for these duties until the 4–4–0 type was introduced. With their stove-pipe chimneys and neat boiler mountings, they strongly suggested contemporary practice on the English Great Eastern Railway, though the railway tended otherwise to model its practice on that of the London and North Western. These 2–4–0s were relatively powerful engines with 18 in. by 24 in. cylinders, 6 ft. diameter coupled wheels and a boiler pressure of 160 lb. per sq. in. Like the great majority of North Western engines, they were coal fired. While the earliest supplies of coal for the Scinde railway were shipped from South Wales, many attempts were made to discover suitable fuel in the territory served by the railway, all to no avail. Eventually a policy was established of purchasing coal from districts east of Delhi served by the East Indian Railway, with consequent long hauls to the N.W.R. depots.

43 Great Northern Railway, England: A Centre-balanced, or 'Somersault' Signal.

In the latter part of the nineteenth century there was general improvement in the design of signalling equipment in Great Britain. This arose partly from failures of earlier, primitive apparatus, which led to accidents, and partly from the need to give more adequate information to the driver,

having regard to the increasing speed of trains. The development of this new type of signal on the Great Northern Railway followed the disastrous double collision at Abbots Ripton in 1876, when signals of the old slotted-post type became clogged with snow, and could not be returned to the danger position. The new design not only had the pivot completely clear of the post, but the arm itself was pivoted at its centre point. If it did become coated with snow it was still balanced. This not only became the standard type of signal on the Great Northern, but was adopted by a number of the local railways in South Wales, and by the Belfast and Northern Counties. It also became standard on several of the Australian State railway systems and in New Zealand. It was certainly a very distinctive 'off' position.

44 London and North Western Railway: New Standard Pressed-Steel Signal Arm.

The L.N.W.R. was one of the many British railways that at one time used the semaphore arm working in a slot in the post, which had proved so dangerous on the Great Northern Railway. On the North Western, however, the change in design was not due to any recognition of danger, but because the manufacture of all signalling apparatus was undertaken at Crewe works, instead of by contractors. Sir Richard Moon, Chairman of the L.N.W.R. was an almost fanatical believer in the principle of 'do it yourself', and gradually more and more variety of work was undertaken in the railway shops. A steel works was established, the company rolled their own rails and an absolute minimum of proprietary articles were embodied in the standard apparatus. At the time signalling was undertaken the standard form of signal arm was a wooden blade; but F. W. Webb constructed this as a steel pressing with longitudinal corrugations to increase the stiffness, and keep weight to a minimum. Tens of thousands of signal arms of this type were made at Crewe.

45 An American Grade-Crossing: The Highball Signals Protecting It.

While the British railways were given great attention to the improvement of their signalling systems and to the apparatus used, there were many thousands of miles in North America operated without any signals other than the written train orders handed to drivers when necessary. The density of traffic did not demand anything more elaborate. In more recent years, coming to a time well beyond the limit of this book, highly sophisticated modern electrical systems have been installed on many lines, completely transforming the old system of working. Yet even today there are picturesque survivals. The author was able to visit and photograph the junction shown in this illustration as recently as 1971. It is a 'level'- or 'grade'-crossing of two single-line routes in the State of Vermont, and the only authorisation for trains to proceed across this intersection is by the raising and lowering of the two red balls. There is no interlocking. The balls can be raised or lowered at will by the conductor of a waiting train acting upon written orders received by the crew.

46 An American Grade-Crossing 'Tower': Novel Interlocking.

In certain cases, when some signalling equipment has been applied to grade-crossings of a similar type to that described under reference 45, signals of the usual American semaphore type have been installed, at an appropriate distance in rear, to protect the crossing, and worked by an orthodox interlocking lever frame. It is very often the case that one or other of the two routes crossing is much more heavily worked than the other, and although the 'Tower' is not normally manned, the signals for that route stand in the clear position for both directions of running. Such a location forms no part of the train order system, and a train would not be stopped to pick up an order. If it were required for a train on the lesser route to cross, the conductor, under instructions, would go to the 'tower', reverse the signals for the conflicting route and clear those for his own train. But to ensure that the signals were not inadvertently left clear for the minor route, the act of putting the major route signals to danger actuates a piece of interlocking that bolts the cabin door. Thus the train conductor cannot get out until his train has passed over the crossing, until he has replaced the signals for the minor route to danger and pulled the major route signals to the clear position.

47 Furness Railway: A Sharp-Stewart 0-6-0 Goods Engine of 1866.

The Furness Railway was essentially a mineral carrier, and it was early in the field with powerful and efficient 0-6-0 locomotives—at least, they were certainly powerful by contemporary standards when they were introduced in 1866. They were so good and so completely reliable that they remained the standard type of goods and mineral engine of the company for nearly 45 years. Although the first batch of 1866 consisted of only 9 engines, another

18 were added in 1871, 12 more in 1873 and a final 6 in 1875. It was not until 1898 that any larger 0–6–0 goods engines were introduced. The 'Sharpies', as engines of the 1866 design were affectionately known, had cylinders 16 in. diameter by 24 in. stroke, coupled wheels 4 ft. 6 in. diameter and a boiler pressure of 120 lb. per sq. in. It was one of these engines that was lost in an extraordinary occurrence at Lindal Moor, in October 1892. The engine was shunting a train of ore wagons when the ground, honeycombed far below with underground mine workings, suddenly caved in. Slowly but surely the engine sank into the hole and by the time the breakdown gang arrived from Barrow she had completely disappeared. Only the little four-wheeled tender was saved. The 'hole' was duly filled in, and trains have run safely over the site ever since; but somewhere in the depths, 200 ft. below the line, are the remains of a 'Sharpie'.

48 London Chatham and Dover Railway: The 'Europa' Class of 2–4–0 Express Passenger Locomotive.

The 'Chatham' may have been bankrupt, and its engineers and operating men forced to scrape and save in every conceivable manner, but when new locomotives were authorised there was no doubt about their quality. The locomotive superintendent, Martley by name, was not only a first-rate engineer, but he had a sense of humour and an irrepressible spirit: so when the construction of one engine was frequently stopped for want of money, when it *was* finished he named it *Enigma*—the 'enigma' being how it ever got finished at all! The 'Europa' class of four locomotives, was built by Sharp, Stewart & Co. in 1873, and was designed for the Continental Mails.

The locomotives were named *Europa*, *Asia*, *Africa* and *America*, and were extremely successful; indeed a distinguished engineering historian considered that they were 'among the most celebrated that ran south of London'—in the nineteenth century, of course. They had cylinders 17 in. diameter by 24 in. stroke; 6 ft. 6 in. coupled wheels, and carried a boiler pressure of 140 lb. per sq. in. Two further engines of the class were built at the railway company's own works at Longhedge, Battersea, in 1876.

49 Highland Railway, Scotland: A 'Skye Bogie' 4–4–0.

Although the Highland Railway penetrated to many remote parts of northern Scotland, it never crossed the sea to Skye, and the origin of the name of these remarkable little engines needs some explanation. It was necessary to provide some communication with the Western Isles from Inverness, and in 1870 what was known as the Dingwall and Skye Railway was opened from a junction with the north main line at Dingwall to Strome Ferry, whence there was a steamer connection to the islands. How the earlier Highland engines struggled over that heavily graded route is scantily recorded, but in 1882 David Jones introduced small-wheeled versions of his standard main-line 4–4–0 specially for this route, and they were immediately referred to by the men as the 'Skye Bogies'. They were robustly built, splendid little engines—ideal for the job—and they remained the standard engines on the line for more than 40 years. There were eight of them in all, with cylinders 18 in. diameter by 24 in. stroke; 5 ft. 3 in. coupled wheels, and boiler pressure of 150 lb. per sq. in.

50 Waterford, Limerick and Western Railway: A 2-4-0 Express Passenger Engine.

This interesting cross-country line, which was absorbed by the Great Southern and Western at just about the turn of the century, was distinguished by a stud of very handsome locomotives. From 1888 the locomotive superintendent was J. G. Robinson, who afterwards built so many handsome engines for the Great Central Railway in England; certainly his Irish engines, of 1888 to 1900, formed a notable series of 'curtain-raisers' to his later work. The 2-4-0 express engine illustrated was one of a class of eight built by Dübs & Co. in Glasgow, between 1889 and 1892. They had a miscellaneous collection of names ranging from that of the Chairman of the company, to Mountains, stately homes and Irish mythology. As can be seen they were neat, handsome and beautifully finished. The cylinders were 17 in. diameter, by 24 in. stroke; the coupled wheels were 6 ft. diameter, and the boiler pressure 150 lb. per sq. in. They did good work on the boat-train runs to and from Waterford, connecting with the English steamers sailing from New Milford. At the same time the 'Waterford Mail' was one of the most important trains on the Great Western Railway in England and Wales.

51 The Westinghouse Brake: The Historic First Test.

In the early days of railways many collisions that could have been prevented or lessened in severity were caused through lack of brake power. Early practice in Great Britain and America was to have brakemen stationed at the front and rear of passenger trains, and a recognised whistle-code by which the driver called for the brakes to be applied. Only the engine and the two brake vans on a long train would be fitted with brakes, and those were applied by hand. In the 1860s George Westinghouse was experimenting with various forms of 'continuous' brake—that is, one by which a brake could be applied on every vehicle in the train—controlled only by the driver. After trying various forms of power he settled upon compressed air, because its use avoided the condensation difficulties that were connected with steam and its propagation down a long pipe through the train.

Like many great inventors Westinghouse had considerable difficulty in interesting the American railways in his proposals. In September 1868 a train equipped with brake apparatus, designed by him and built, not only under his supervision, but partly with his own hands, began its initial trip from the Union Station in Pittsburg. It had to pass through Grants Hill Tunnel, and just as the locomotive came into the open again, rapidly gathering speed, a cart drawn by two horses appeared on the level-crossing immediately ahead. With the equipment formerly in use, nothing could have prevented a collision on that crossing, particularly as the terrified animals became unmanageable. But the driver of the train closed the throttle and made a full application of the air brake; and the train stopped safely, inches clear of the cart. There could not have been a finer advertisement for the new brake. The news of the incident became front-page news in every city of the U.S.A., and American railways could not get the Westinghouse brake fast enough.

2 **The 'Last Spike':** The Historic Ceremonial Completion of the Canadian Pacific Railway.

The years 1881–85 were momentous ones in the history of Canada. In those four years the great trans-continental railway was carried through to the Pacific coast. As in the famous 'Golden Spike' episode in the U.S.A. in 1869, constructional parties were working eastwards and westwards, but in this case it was only one railway, the Canadian Pacific. The 'meet' took place early in the morning of 7 November 1885, in the Eagle Pass, British Columbia. It was a completely simple occasion: no 'golden spike', no 'golden' oratory. Just a couple of 'business cars' carrying senior officials and a very few guests. The general manager, William Cornelius Van Horne had said previously that the last spike would be 'just as good an iron one as there is between Montreal and Vancouver, and anyone who wants to see it driven will have to pay full fare'! The spike was driven by Donald A. Smith, afterwards Lord Strathcona, and in the group watching the act were the famous pioneer surveyor Sandford Fleming, in the tall hat, with snow-white beard, and Van Horne himself, just on Fleming's right. Today there is no station at the spot; but it is named Craigellachie, and marked by a cairn.

53 **Broad Street Station, Philadelphia:** Pennsylvania Railroad.

This great station, built in 1893, for many years ranked as one of the world's most famous. The illustration shows the immense span of the single-arched roof extended to 300 ft. 8 in. It covered 16 tracks, and a similar number of platform faces, and as the illustration suggests it was a terminus—what the Americans term a 'stub-ended layout'. At the time it was built, transport facilities in the streets were somewhat meagre, and although traffic normally flowed north and south through the city area, and west of the Schuylkill River, it was thought desirable to locate the station near the business centre. So the station was built almost a mile east of the river, and at West Philadelphia through express trains had to turn through a right angle, and proceed over the mile to Broad Street Terminus. After completing station business and attaching a fresh engine at what had been the rear of the train, they had to retrace steps westward across the river and then once again turn through a right angle to resume their direction, north or south as the case might be. In June 1923, however, the great roof was destroyed by fire, and with the changed traffic situation in the city itself an entirely new station layout was designed and built at West Philadelphia.

54 **A Characteristic American Locomotive Shed:** The 'Roundhouse'.

In the earliest days of railways, the almost universal way of housing locomotives that were not in use was in the picturesque 'roundhouse'. One can refer to it in the past tense so far as Great Britain and countries following British practice are concerned, though it has remained standard practice in North America and on the continent of Europe. It was very convenient to have locomotives parked on tracks radiating from a central turntable. They could be serviced under cover, while standing over a pit, and then brought out to take the road when required. The 'roundhouse' began to fall out of favour in

Great Britain as locomotives spent a smaller part of their time actually 'on shed'. When it became necessary to secure the highest utilisation from the stock, the idea of having locomotives tucked neatly inside sheds did not fit in with changing philosophies, and the 'through' shed began to take its place. In this latter, engines arriving went in at one end, were duly attended to, and moved sequentially towards the leaving end, spending a minimum of time 'on shed'. But a through shed is a highly utilitarian affair compared to a 'roundhouse'. One of the most picturesque of British roundhouses was that of the Highland Railway, at Inverness, which had an ornamental water tower over the track leading to the central turntable.

55 Chicago and North Western Railway: Bridge across the Wisconsin River at Merrimac.

The Chicago and North Western was one of the great railways of the U.S.A. formed out of many amalgamations and extensions in the latter part of the nineteenth century. In its advance to the north west through the state of Wisconsin it had to cross the Wisconsin River, an important tributary of the Mississippi, which great river forms the western boundary of the state. The fine bridge illustrated was opened on 1879; but it carried only a single line of rails, and as the traffic developed it had to be replaced by a more modern structure. The original bridge, however, provides a most interesting example of earlier American design of bridge construction in the massive stone piers supporting the girders spanning three parts of the river that are not navigable, and the large 'through' box girder for the central span. It will be seen that the 'deck' girders forming the landward spans have

the 'tie' members made up of a series of rods, while the struts are necessarily solid fabricated assemblies. In common with usual North American practice, which prevails generally today, the deck-girder part of the bridge has no parapets. It certainly gives an odd feeling when one is crossing in the driver's cab of a modern diesel locomotive!

56 Paris, Lyons and Mediterranean Railway: Monte Carlo station.

The Côte d'Azur is one of the most picturesque stretches of coastline in Europe, quite apart from the fame of the various resorts, the names of which are household words. The railway from Marseilles to the Italian frontier runs near to the coast for much of the way, particularly on the most easterly stretch, where the Maritime Alps rise straight from the sea, and the line is carried on ledges and in tunnels high above the immediate water's edge. Until quite recently there was a most dramatic stretch, within sight of the rock of Monaco, where the line made its way on sharp curves immediately above the harbour to the rock ledge, on which is built the world-famous casino of Monte Carlo; and immediately beneath the gardens of the casino was the railway station. The old picturesque, nineteenth-century station illustrated remained in use until no more than a few years ago, when the old line was replaced by a tunnel beneath the town. However improved the railways may be, with the line electrified, travellers by train are now deprived of the breathtaking view of the rock of Monaco across the harbour and, as the train leaves for the east, the magnificent view of the coastal range of mountains ahead.

57 Austrian Northern Railway: 2–2–2 Express Passenger Locomotive of 1873.

In the previous volume of this series *The Dawn of Railways 1800–1850* the exceptional haulage problems of the steeply graded line over the Semmering Pass were described, and the various special types of locomotives proposed were illustrated. In contrast to that route, however, there were many territories within the Austro-Hungarian Empire where the running was level, and an interesting and picturesque 2–2–2 'single' built for the 'Nordbahn', illustrated here, provides a striking contrast to the mountain-climbing types tried out on the Semmering Pass. The design of outside framing is interesting. The deep section, with large slotted holes, is typical of Austrian practice of the period; but it is noteworthy that the leading pair of wheels also have outside frames, although ensconced behind the cylinder and slide bars. 'Express' passenger engines were something of a rarity in Austria at that time, and the one illustrated was the first ever built by the famous firm of Wiener Lokomotivfabrik.

58 Austrian Southern Railway: 2–4–0 Passenger Locomotive of 1873.

This line, the Südbahn, ran southwards from Vienna over level country to the foothills of the eastern ranges of the Alps, through which the railway made its way into Styria via the Semmering Pass. The 2–4–0 locomotive illustrated, also built by the Wiener Lokomotivfabrik, is strongly reminiscent, so far as the boiler is concerned, of the Stephenson long-boilered type in England. The firebox is relatively small and deep, and accommodated

entirely in the rear of the after-pair of coupled wheels. This design was generally favoured by 'Wiener' in their early days. One sees also the same form of outside framing, and the machinery outside is complicated by the link motion working direct to valves mounted in a chest immediately above the cylinder. Another interesting feature is the huge diameter of the leading pair of wheels. Diamond-shaped smoke stacks incorporating spark-arresting apparatus were common on the continent of Europe at that period, as can be seen from the Swiss locomotive *Genf* (ref. 71). The further development of motive power on the Austrian Südbahn can be followed in a companion volume, *Railways at the Turn of the Century 1895–1905*, with the 4–4–0-type locomotive.

59 Austrian North-Western Railway: 4–4–0 Passenger Locomotive of 1873.

There was clearly little in the way of standardisation in locomotive design between the various Government-owned and private railways of the Austro-Hungarian Empire in the latter part of the nineteenth century. If one compares the locomotives illustrated under references 58 and 59, it could be inferred that they are intended for the same kind of work. The boiler proportions are similar, the outside framing is the same and the cylinder and outside valve-gear layout looks virtually identical. But then the differences in detail come crowding in. The Nordwestbahn provided the important main line between Vienna and Prague, a route over which the stately Gölsdorf four-cylinder compound 2–6–4s ran in later years, and the locomotive illustrated had a short-wheelbase, leading bogie instead of the single pair of large-diameter, leading wheels on the Südbahn engine. The cab appeared to be more commodious, though the overhanging firebox protruded far into it, and the plain chimney, with an ornamental rim at the bottom as well as the top, was the same design as that of the Nordbahn 'single' (ref. 57).

60 Austrian North-Western Railway: 4-4-0 Express Passenger Locomotive of 1874.

When this railway augmented its motive power stud by the addition of the *Schnellzuglokomotive* to the previous, more general service, *Personenzug Lokomotive*, the requirements of faster running brought a complete change in design. In Austria, as in England and everywhere else, the Stephenson long-boilered type of locomotive proved unstable at express speed; and although the provision of a four-wheeled bogie at the front end probably improved the riding of the Nordwestbahn engine, reference 59, in comparison with the Südbahn 2-4-0, the grouping of the wheels all together ahead of the firebox did not eliminate the tendency for a 'yawing' action to develop at speed. In the true 'express' locomotive illustrated there is a long-wheelbase bogie, and the coupled wheels are moved towards the rear end, with the firebox set deep between the two coupled axles, as in British practice of the same period. The cylinders have been moved back to drive on the rear pair of coupled wheels, and the valve gear is still accommodated entirely outside. The picturesque outside frames have been replaced by inside frames, and a characteristic feature of many Continental locomotives —the hinged lid over the chimney—appears for the first time. On all these Austrian locomotives the valve gear outside is the Allan straight-link motion.

61 Midland Railway, England: A 'Kirtley' 0-6-0 Goods Engine of 1868.

The year 1868 was that in which the Midland Railway extension to its terminus at St. Pancras was opened. There was simultaneously a marked increase in freight traffic, and in that year a powerful new class of 0-6-0 locomotives was introduced by Matthew Kirtley, the locomotive superintendent. The first twenty were built in Glasgow, by Dübs & Co., and a further ten came from the Yorkshire Engine Co. in 1869. They were splendid examples of locomotive construction; with their massive outside frames and generous bearing surfaces they were ideal for the heavy work they had to do. They had $16\frac{1}{4}$ in. by 24 in. cylinders; coupled wheels 5 ft. 2 in. diameter. The illustration shows one of them in the green livery current at the time of their introduction, also with the Kirtley style of chimney, boiler mountings and plain, curved weatherboard 'cab'. In later years they were re-boilered by S. W. Johnson, fitted with cabs and in due course were repainted Midland 'red'. The majority of these 30 engines had a life-span of more than 60 years. Four of them were not withdrawn until 1932, and one lasted until 1946, seventy-seven years after it was constructed!

62 Great Southern and Western Railway, Ireland: 2-4-0 Express Passenger Locomotive.

The Great Southern and Western, during the latter part of the nineteenth century, modelled its locomotive practice very much upon that of the London and North Western, and the 2–4–0 express engine illustrated bore a remarkable likeness to John Ramsbottom's 'Newton' class, of which the first example was built at Crewe in 1866. On the G.S. & W.R. Alexander McDonnell's 'copy' was produced at Inchicore Works, Dublin, in 1869. The Irish engines were, of course, built for the standard 5 ft. 3 in. gauge, though they were actually less powerful than their English counterparts, having cylinders only 16 in. diameter, instead of 17 in. There were six of the Irish 2–4–0s, and they were used on the mail trains between Dublin and Cork. The engine illustrated was the latest development of this general class, of which two examples were built in 1875 specially for the mails, which had then been accelerated. These two engines had 17 in. cylinders like the Crewe 'Newton' class. No more 2–4–0 passenger engines were built for the G.S. & W.R., and after McDonnell had gone to the North Eastern Railway in 1884 his successor built nothing but 4–4–0s for express traffic. A beautiful model of one of the McDonnell 2–4–0s is displayed in a glass case at the Institution of Mechanical Engineers in London.

63 Great Northern Railway, England: A 'Stirling' Eight-Footer.

The influence of Archibald Shurrock's work on the Great Northern Railway on subsequent French practice is mentioned later in this book (ref. 101–104), while under reference 33 the changes in boiler practice at Doncaster, wrought by his successor, are mentioned. Patrick Sterling was one of the great artist-engineers of nineteenth-century England—as distinctive and original in his work as Stroudley and

William Adams. One feels sometimes, indeed, that Stirling carried artistry a little beyond the realms of practical engineering. Certainly his 8-ft. bogie singles were masterpieces of locomotive lineament, in the combination of outside cylinders, the graceful sweep of the running plate over the driving wheel boss, so that the action of the connecting rod was completely in view all the time, and above all the magnificently fashioned cover over the safety valves. Technically, the engines had rather small boilers in relation to the size of the cylinders. The latter were 18 in. by 28 in. on the earliest engines of the class dating from 1870, increased to no less than 19½ in. diameter on the final batch of 1894–5. They were extremely reliable engines, though naturally limited in the loads that they could haul. The pioneer engine of the class, No. 1, is preserved in the railway museum at York.

64 Manchester, Sheffield and Lincolnshire Railway: A 'Sacré' 4–4–0 of 1878.

The M.S. & L. was to a large extent a mineral carrier connecting the Yorkshire coalfield with East Lancashire by an exceedingly severe route across the Pennines. At the summit was the notorious Woodhead Tunnel, in which conditions on heavily worked engines were made much worse by there being two single-line bores, instead of a much larger one for double line. East of Sheffield however the company was called upon to do some fast running. The M.S. & L. was in partnership with the Great Northern running a highly competitive service between London and Manchester; and the M.S. & L. provided the motive power as far south as Grantham. Charles Sacré, the locomotive superintendent, introduced his celebrated '423' class of 4–4–0 in 1878, and the 27 engines of this class did most of the express working on the line, until some new outside-cylindered 2–2–2s were built specially for the London trains east of Sheffield. The Sacré 4–4–0s had 17 in. by 26 in. cylinders, 6 ft. 3 in. coupled wheels and carried a boiler pressure of 140 lb. per sq. in. The outside framing was unusual in that the slotted frame was carried forward to the front buffer beam, although it had no physical connection with the bogie.

65 The Anhalter Station, Berlin.

The 'sixties' and 'seventies' of last century were an interesting period in railway architecture. Most of the great British stations were then completed, and extensions, or rebuildings, were strictly utilitarian rather than containing any particular artistic merit. This was probably due to the sites having become closely encompassed by other buildings, which would have obscured any noble vistas an architect might have envisaged. On the continent of Europe, however, the example of the great British stations began to be noted to the extent that when many of the early train sheds demanded enlargement some distinctive architectural styles were embodied in the façades. This trend was shown no more markedly than in Germany, and culminated in the magnificent Anhalter station. Here the architect was Franz Schwechten, and his work is considered by some to be the finest terminal station frontage in Europe. It has been justifiably praised for the impression created upon an intending traveller, who could see at a glance how he should proceed. The entrance porch, projecting forward, invited him in, the waiting rooms lay conveniently on either side once he had entered, while

behind soared the vast curvilinear mass of the 'train shed'.

66 St. Pancras Station, London: Midland Railway, 1868.

The Midland Railway originally obtained access to London by the exercise of running powers over the Great Northern for a distance of 32 miles from Hitchin to King's Cross. But it was no more than a temporary, and highly inconvenient arrangement, and in 1868 the London extension of the Midland from Bedford was completed. As a new competitor entering London, the Midland Railway determined to have a terminal station of distinctive architectural quality, and the combined efforts of Sir Gilbert Scott as architect and W. H. Barlow as engineer certainly produced an outstanding result. The conventional distinction between 'wall' and 'ceiling' was abolished, for the ribs of the great Gothic-shaped roof continue in an unbroken line from platform level until they meet at the ridge. The platforms are, in fact, in the roof, and there are two lower storeys of this great building used for purposes quite otherwise than railway traffic. The actual dimensions are impressive. The 'shed' is 243 ft. wide, 600 ft. long and the point of the arch is 100 ft. above rail level. Contemporary architectural testimonials, in all parts of the world, mingled awe with admiration; it was generally considered one of the greatest achievements of the century.

67 York Station: North Eastern Railway of England.

York is a striking example of a station adapted to changing circumstances of railway travel. The first railway to enter the city was the York and North Midland, which came in from the south, through an arch in the city wall to an unpretentious terminus just short of the right bank of the River Ouse. Then came the Great North of England, also skirting the right bank of the river. The two had inevitably to be connected to provide through communication from north to south, and an entirely new station was built on a considerable curve. Two eminent architects were employed, William Peachey and Thomas Prosser, and although the exterior is not particularly distinguished, they contrived a remarkably handsome effect in the huge, concentrically curved 'train sheds'. The five-centred ribs are carefully scaled and the tie-rods barely noticeable. The station has been considerably enlarged, by provision of additional platforms on the inner side of the concentric system; but these lie outside the original train shed of 1877, and have modern awnings of quite nondescript character. With the tremendous sweep of the original curved roof, York still remains one of the most striking railway stations in the world.

68 **Worcester, Massachusetts:** The Union Station of 1877.

This very striking edifice, a contemporary of York, was generally considered one of the most picturesque ever erected in the U.S.A. Yet in its design the architects, Ware and Van Brunt, had many restrictions placed upon them. Some trains entered the 'shed' obliquely, while others went straight through, and there was thus only one corner where the administrative buildings could be placed. A contemporary description states that the 'head-house', as it is termed in the U.S.A., was partly slid in under the shed and partly projected

from the corner. The architects wanted to make the great tower even higher, but the directors would not authorise the additional expense purely for decorative purposes. But with this limitation, a magnificent ensemble was achieved, with tower, the rounded 'head-house' and the sheds faced in stone. The 'sheds' were actually iron, and the stone facing was purely an adornment. But in contrast to the extensively glazed roofs of St. Pancras and York, this American station must have been very dark inside. The station was demolished when the layout had to be enlarged, but the tower was retained as a historical relic.

69 **Sorocabana Railroad, Brazil:** A 2–8–0 Freight Locomotive of 1889.

The Sorocabana Railroad was an amalgamation of several one-time independent lines, and then consisted of a series of routes running westwards and south-westwards from São Paulo. One of these constituents was the Huana Railway, and it was for this line that the locomotive illustrated was originally built. It was peculiar in having a rail gauge of 3 ft. 1¾ in., though after the various amalgamations, the gauge was unified at one metre. The photograph on which the illustration was based was taken when the locomotive was 39 years old, and still practically unaltered from the original condition. A number of locomotives on other Brazilian railways were also burning wood at the time, and the balloon stack and tenders with high-railed supports for the logs were not then the curiosities that they might otherwise be considered. They were quite small engines, with cylinders 15 in. diameter by 18 in. stroke, coupled wheels 3 ft. 1 in. diameter and carried a boiler pressure of only 130 lb. per sq. in. The total weight of the engine only, in working order, was 28 tons. They were built by the Baldwin Locomotive Company in U.S.A.

70 Andalusian Railways: 0–6–0 Goods Engine of 1877.

These 'dumpy' little engines, of which a total of 25 was put into service between 1877 and 1901, were the mainstay of the intermediate freight motive power of the Andalusian Railway. Indeed, until quite recently a number of them were still on their old duties of pick-up goods and shunting work. They were powerful engines at the time of their introduction, having cylinders $17\frac{3}{4}$ in. diameter by $25\frac{1}{2}$ in. stroke and coupled wheels 4 ft. 3 in. diameter. Their outward appearance could be described as French, though actually all except two of them were built by Hartmann, at Chemnitz, Germany. The other two were built in Russia. Until quite recently they could be seen at work around Cadiz, Cordoba and Algeciras, and a visitor entering Spain from a steamer at Algeciras would most likely have had his first sight of a Spanish locomotive in one of these little veterans shunting on the quayside. They were also engaged in light passenger and mixed trains right down to the 1960s. Nevertheless, the tempo of railway operation in Andalusia is not exactly brisk, and their long lives may well have been equally a measure of their gentle treatment as of their good design and construction.

71 Swiss Central Railway: 0–4–6 Tank Engine, *Genf*, of 1858.

This remarkable engine, built by Kessler at Esslingen in 1858, was used for hauling the train of the official party at the opening of the Hauenstein line of the Swiss Central Railway. But quite apart from its original usage the design of the engine had some very unusual features. It was built on the Engerth system, developed by an Austrian engineer of that name, and used a part of the loaded tender to augment the adhesion weight. It will be seen that the water tanks were carried well forward and extended over the rear pair of coupled wheels. The rear end was pivoted, and this part carried more water and all the coal. Because of this pivoting of the rear end it could not strictly be called a 'tank engine', and the German word of description can be translated as 'supported tenders'. The Swiss Central Railway at one time had 60 locomotives on the Engerth system. Some of these were 0–4–6s, like *Genf*; some were 0–4–4s and others 0–6–4s. *Genf* is preserved in the Swiss Railway Museum at Lucerne. She had an active life of 40 years and fortunately was not scrapped after her withdrawal from traffic in 1898.

72 Madrid, Zaragoza and Alicante Railway: An 0–8–0 Goods Engine of 1878.

Except for the large, extended cab-roof, and the four-wheeled tender, this could be recognised as an English locomotive. It was, in fact, one of a class built by Sharp, Stewart & Co. of Manchester in 1878–80, and was generally in advance of any freight locomotive that had been constructed for the British home railways up to that time. There had been one or two isolated, and unsuccessful, attempts to use the 0–8–0 type, but it was not until F. W. Webb introduced it on the London and North Western Railway in 1892 that it began to assume importance as a standard, heavy-freight locomotive. The Spanish engines delivered when the railway was the

'Tarragona–Barcelona–Francia', were massive things, having cylinders 20 in. diameter by 26 in. stroke, and a coupled wheel diameter of 4 ft. 6½ in. They had inside Stephenson's link motion, and the standard British details of construction at that time. They were all in service until the mid-1960s, with some working in the Tarragona area on shunting duties. This earlier series of 0–8–0s was much better looking than the later ones from Sharp, Stewart, because the sandboxes were mounted, as shown, on the running plate instead of on top of the boiler.

73 New South Wales Government Railways: The Great Zig-Zag.

The early railway engineers in highly mountainous districts were faced with a two-fold problem—that of surmounting great escarpments, or steps in deep valleys created by glacial action in the past, and yet keeping constructional costs to a minimum because funds were limited. John Whitton, engineer of the New South Wales Government Railways, had such a problem in carrying the main west line from Sydney across the precipitous ridges of the Blue Mountains. To avoid tunnelling as far as possible, he adopted a zig-zag location up the face of the escarpment. Trains would climb the first incline, reach a reversing station and then be propelled up the next section before reversing direction again for the final ascent. It was a slow and inconvenient way of working, but was used from 1869, until the traffic demanded the doubling of the line, and a new alignment. It is amply indicative of the costs that were avoided in the first place when it is added that the new line, avoiding the Zig-Zag, includes no fewer than *ten* tunnels. The original Zig-Zag has

been re-constituted as a road, along which one can drive and see the remarkable engineering.

74 The Gotthard Line, Switzerland: Spiral Tunnels near Giornico.

In construction of the great 'north to south' railway through the Gotthard pass, the Swiss engineers were working in very different conditions from John Whitton in New South Wales. The Gotthard line was planned as a major traffic artery from the start. One would not go so far as to say that unlimited funds were available, but the purse was a great deal deeper than in Australia. Not only was a great tunnel over 9 miles long to be driven under the St. Gotthard pass itself, but two mighty 'ramps' had to be constructed on the approach lines from north and south. No ordinary gradients could be provided, since the line was going to be steam-operated. On both sides of the central *massif* the line was taken up these wild valleys through a series of spiral tunnels. Both at Wassen on the north side, and at Giornico on the south, two long spirals were constructed so that one could see three levels of the railway, one above the other. The gradient was kept down to 1 in 38, and although this naturally proved trying to steam locomotives it has been shorn of its difficulties by electric traction. The powerful locomotives now in use on the line haul the heaviest trains at the maximum speeds permitted on the spirals, namely 47 m.p.h.

75 Midland Railway, Settle and Carlisle Line: Arten Gill Viaduct.

The decision of the Midland Railway to build its own independent line from Hellifield, Yorkshire, to the Scottish Border involved the company's engineers and contractors in some of the heaviest construction work to be seen anywhere in England. The line was planned as a high-speed express route, and although it ran through 75 miles of the wildest mountain country no liberties were taken with the landscape to save costs. The line had to be straight, and of uniform grading; and if there was an obstruction in the way, or a deep valley to be crossed, only one method was acceptable—to blast through the obstacle, or to continue on an evenly graded course across the valley. There were some very long tunnels, some very deep cuttings blasted out of the solid rock and some lofty, magnificently picturesque viaducts. Arten Gill viaduct comes on a most dramatic stretch of the line, when the railway is being carried immensely high on a shoulder of the hills flanking Dentdale, North Yorkshire. Every third pier is made exceptionally massive, and the masonry work constructed in the local stone blends superbly with the wild moorland landscape. The line was opened for traffic in 1876.

76 The Forth Bridge, Scotland: The Towers Under Construction.

One could well claim that the Forth Bridge is still the most famous bridge in the world. It is also one of the most beautiful. Until it was built in 1891, trains by the East Coast Route from Edinburgh to the North had to travel by way of Stirling to reach Dundee. Such was the keenness of competition between the East and West Routes to Perth and Aberdeen that the East Coast companies—the Great Northern, North Eastern and North British—entered into partnership with the Midland Railway to finance the construction of a great bridge across the Firth of Forth. Although the Midland was not one of the East Coast

companies, it operated through carriages from various English cities to Perth, Aberdeen and Inverness, and stood to gain considerably from the acceleration of service that the bridge would make possible. The four railways formed the Forth Bridge Railway Company. The bridge itself was built on the cantilever principle, constructing the central towers, as shown in this illustration, and extending the steelwork out from each, in complete balance, to meet the steelwork extending from the adjoining tower. This great bridge was opened in 1891, and immediately gave the East Coast route an advantage in the distance from London to Aberdeen of $16\frac{1}{2}$ miles over the West Coast, 523·2 miles against 539·7.

77 Baden Railways: A Passenger Train Brake Van.

The average passenger train on the continent of Europe during the later part of the nineteenth century presented a remarkably variegated appearance in the different shapes and sizes of successive vehicles in the train. This was the case to an even greater extent with some of the principal international services such as those running from the Channel Ports of Holland or Belgium. These attached and detached, en route, through carriages of various nationalities. Some would be of the latest bogie type; but there was a liberal admixture of four-wheeled and six-wheeled stock extending even to the older types of sleeping car. The highly functional brake van illustrated is typical of the kind of vehicle one might find in the middle of an international express train. The lengthy wheelbase will be noted, but an interesting feature is the small iron fences on the roof. These were to protect the roof lights from lamp men and others whose duty it might be to walk along the roofs. The high-raised box for the brakeman was a prominent feature.

78 Jura–Simplon Railway, Switzerland: A Six-Wheeled First- and Second-Class Composite Carriage.

To the great majority of travellers today the Jura–Simplon line is a great international highway followed by some of the most famous named trains of the world. As its name suggests the line extends from the Jura mountains on the north-western frontiers of Switzerland to the Simplon Pass, travelling for most of the way beside the Lake of Geneva, and then up the Rhône valley. Until the year 1906, however, the Jura–Simplon was not a through route at all, and terminated at Brigue, set deep among the mountains of the Valais. It was for this important, though purely Swiss, route that the type of carriage illustrated was introduced in 1889. There was seating for 12 first-class and 24 second-class passengers, with lavatories in the centre of the vehicle. Rather forbidding outside, the interior was nicely furnished for both classes, and equipped with electric light. Entrance was only at the ends, and at the time it was the rule on Swiss railways for the doors to be locked after the train had started. Just before each stop, the travelling porters came along and unlocked the doors, at the same time shouting the name of the station that was being approached.

79 New South Wales Government Railways: A Passenger Carriage of the 1880s.

The evolution of passenger carriages on the railways of New South Wales followed very much on the English pattern at first.

The early four-wheelers provided roomy and fairly comfortable accommodation for first-class passengers, but the earliest 'thirds' were, as in England, little better than covered wagons, with large openings between the waist-line and the roof instead of windows.

The first eight-wheeled carriages came out from England in 1869, and were a great improvement upon earlier patterns; but the real advance began in 1877 with the first introduction of true bogie coaches. The illustration shows a typical carriage of the 1880s, constructed entirely in timber on the compartment style then almost universal in England, and having straight-up backs to the seats. It will be seen that the 'double' form of roof was employed, as used on some of the early Japanese carriages. It was a relatively light and cramped vehicle to seat 60 third-class passengers. The lighting was by incandescent gas.

80 Central Pacific Railroad: A Typical Freight Train 'Caboose'.

The Central Pacific formed the western end of the first trans-continental railway across the U.S.A. and continued from Promontory, Utah, when the famous Golden Spike ceremony was staged (refs. 15 and 16), to San Francisco. On the railways of North America the caboose has of necessity always been much more than the humble 'guards van' of the British goods train. It was not only the control point of the train conductor, but it provided living quarters on a long run, and had comprehensive, if simple, facilities for cooking en route. A North American freight train carries at least five in the crew. In addition to the driver, the fireman and the conductor, there is a front and a rear brakeman, and the rear brakeman would usually travel in the caboose. On heavy gradients when a 'pusher' locomotive was assisting in rear it was very often the practice to detach the caboose, marshall the pusher locomotive immediately behind the last wagon and have the caboose trailing behind the pusher locomotive. In our illustration can be seen the large 'possum belly', as it was termed, used for storing tools and gear.

81 Chicago, Rock Island and Pacific: The 'Silver' 4–4–0 Locomotive, *America*.

In this book, and in the previous volume in this series, *The Dawn of World Railways 1800–1850*, there have been frequent references to the adornment of early locomotives on the railways of the U.S.A. in gay colours and a variety of decorative devices, but the *America*, built in 1867 by the Grant Locomotive Works, has been described as the 'showiest engine ever rolled off the Grant erecting floor'. She was not built to the order of the 'Rock Island', but was shipped immediately to France, to the Universal Exposition in Paris. There she won the highest awards. All the fittings and the entire boiler jacket were of the finest quality German silver, and her cab was described as a masterpiece of the joiner's art, inlaid with select hardwood. On her return to the U.S.A. she was purchased by the Chicago, Rock Island and Pacific, became No. 109 of that railroad and retained the name, *America*. In May 1869, she worked the inaugural train into Council Bluffs, Iowa, and two years later established herself as something of a 'flyer' on the Chicago–Omaha mail service on which the railway was then in keen competition. It is said that during that exciting period her driver was a stripling of 19

years! The illustration shows beautiful scroll work put on to splashers and tender, and the ornamental castings on the front of the smokebox saddle.

82 Delaware, Lackawanna and Western Railroad: An Outstanding 'American'-type Locomotive.

In the early days of railways in the U.S.A., there was considerable diversity in gauges, though the situation never reached the crisis point that developed in England at the height of Great Western advocacy of the 7-ft. gauge. Nevertheless the Lackawanna persisted in its use of the 6-ft. gauge until the year 1876. In that year, however, a change was made to the standard 4 ft. $8\frac{1}{2}$ in. and many new locomotives were purchased. Among these were some 4–4–0s for fast passenger traffic. These were of the standard 'American' type; but towards the end of the period of this book they were extensively rebuilt with the wide Wootten-type firebox then coming into great favour in the U.S.A. It is in this form that the engine, *W. F. Hallstead*, is illustrated. In the rebuilding, a 'Mother Hubbard' type of cab has been fitted, and it would seem that this latter change was made as much because the width of the firebox precluded the use of an ordinary cab as to improve the driver's look-out. Cab position or not, the engines of this class did very good work for a number of years. They had cylinders $18\frac{1}{2}$ in. in diameter by 24 in. stroke, coupled wheels 5 ft. 9 in. diameter and carried a boiler pressure of 160 lb. per sq. in. The class was not withdrawn until 1921.

83 Louisville and Nashville Railroad: A 'Ten-Wheeler' of 1890.

The Louisville and Nashville can trace its origins back to the very early days of

American railroading. Like the Lackawanna it was proposed as a 6 ft. gauge line; but only 2½ miles of this track was laid, in 1854, and it was then continued on the 5-ft. gauge. During the American Civil War it was in the thick of the fighting, and suffered much damage; but after peace was restored a big programme of expansion was undertaken, still on the 5-ft. gauge. During this period the standard type of locomotive was the 'American', and large numbers of highly ornamental examples were put to work. The gauge remained 5 ft. until 1886, and by that time the loads of the more important trains were getting beyond the hauling capacity of 4–4–0s. So there was a change to the 4–6–0, or 'ten-wheeler'. The engine illustrated was one of a batch purchased from the Rogers Locomotive Works in 1890, and represented an advance in traction power of some 33 per cent over the most powerful of the 4–4–0s. An interesting feature, becoming standard then on the majority of L & N locomotives, was the Belpaire firebox, though this is not readily discernible because most of its length was inside the cab. These engines had 20 in. by 24 in. cylinders; 5 ft. 7 in. wheels and boiler pressure of 175 lb. per sq. in.

84 Central Pacific Railroad: The *El Gobernado*, a 4–10–0 of 1883.

The Central Pacific will always be famous in railway history as one of the two companies racing to complete the transcontinental line across the U.S.A., leading to the famous 'Golden Spike' ceremony at Promontory Utah (refs. 15 and 16). But in 1883, motive power developments had moved rapidly from the little *Jupiter* which represented the company in 1869. The heavy gradients in the Sierra Nevada

mountains had demanded more powerful engines for freight, and in 1882 the Master Mechanic of the railroad, A. J. Stevens, built an experimental 4–8–0 at the Sacramento shops. It was very successful, and 20 more were added to the stock. Then Stevens went one better, and built the so-called 'iron monster', the *El Gobernado*. At that time it was the largest locomotive in the world. The cylinders were 21 in. diameter by 36 in. stroke; the coupled wheels were 4 ft. 9 in. diameter, and the weight of the engine alone in working order, 65 tons. But the track was not ready for this great engine. Trestles had to be strengthened, part of the line re-railed, and the engine did very little work. But she remained a prestige symbol and was steamed up on numerous special occasions for display purposes. Her most unusual feature was, of course, the exceptional length of piston stroke, 36 in., of which the length of the cylinder shown in the illustration is ample evidence.

85 Caledonian Railway: 0–4–4 Tank Engine for the Cathcart Circle Line.

Although the London area is often considered to provide some of the most intense suburban working in the world, certain other British cities had their problems too, and one of these was the Cathcart Circle line in South Glasgow. This was not a circle in the same sense as the Inner Circle on the London Underground system, but a line on which trains departed from Glasgow Central station, went either clockwise or anti-clockwise round the 'circle', and terminated again in the Central station. The intermediate stations are very close together; gradients are steep and curves severe, so that a locomotive of high accelerative capacity was needed. The locomotive superintendent of the Caledonian Railway, J. F. McIntosh, had introduced a very successful class of 0-4-4 tank engine for general short distance working; these had coupled wheels of 5 ft. 9 in. diameter, and had a fine turn of speed; but for the Cathcart Circle, to give the rapid acceleration required, he used wheels of no more than 4 ft. 6 in. They were powerful and efficient little engines, and put in more than 30 years of work on this strenuous but unspectacular duty.

86 Victorian Railways: 'E' Class 2-4-2 Suburban Tank Engine.

Among railways in far-overseas countries of the British Empire those of Victoria were at one time the most English of them all. Locomotives were gorgeously arrayed in liveries that rivalled the most ornate of nineteenth-century 'home rails', but even then, in many line services, there were necessary additions, such as cowcatchers, and large canopied cabs to protect the men from the rays of the fierce Australian sun. Around Melbourne, however, a remarkably busy suburban traffic was growing up. There was an intricate network of branch lines, some on steep gradients, feeding into the great central station of Flinders Street; and on these trains were used some very smart little 2-4-2 tank engines. They had no need for cow-catchers, and their cabs extended as usual, with the result that they could literally have been mistaken for an English design. They were as good as their appearance was handsome, and they worked the entire suburban service until 1908, when the 4-6-2 tanks were introduced. One of these little 2-4-2 tanks has been preserved, and is to be seen in the railway museum at North Williamstown, near Melbourne.

87 Great Indian Peninsula Railway: An 0-8-0 Saddle-Tank Engine for Ghat Incline.

The 'G.I.P.', to give it the familiar description of 40 years ago, was the first railway to be promoted in India. Its Act of Incorporation, indeed, dates back to 1849. But while its first sections of line were laid in the level country immediately to the east of Bombay, it had, like all early railways in India an eventual importance of strategic purposes, and the aim was to provide railway communication between Bombay, the port of arrival in India of passengers, troops and supplies from England, and the cities in the valley of the Ganges. Immediately inland from Bombay lies the formidable mountain range of the Western Ghats. The escarpments were at one time thought to be inaccessible, until the zig-zag form of incline was considered by James Berkley. Then separate zig-zags were constructed for the main routes to Calcutta and Madras, but even so the gradients were as steep as 1 in 37. To provide rear-end banking assistance on the Ghat Inclines, the G.I.P. Railway introduced the massive 0-8-0 saddle-tank engines illustrated. They were built by Neilson & Co. in Glasgow, and had cylinders 18 in. diameter by 26 in. stroke, 4 ft. diameter coupled wheels and weighed 59 tons in working order. The gauge of the railway is the Indian broad-gauge standard of 5 ft. 6 in.

88 Mexican Central Railway: A Mason–Fairlie Articulated 2-6-6 Tank Locomotive.

The principal of the articulated locomotive first demonstrated by Robert Fairlie, and made for ever famous in the 'double-engines' of the Festiniog Railway in North Wales (ref. 25) led to a number of variations introduced by many locomotive engineers in different parts of the world. One of these inventors was William Mason, of Taunton, Massachusetts. In his variation the main frames of the locomotive swivelled under the boiler, so that the locomotive was supported on two 'bogies'. The forward 'bogie' included the driving wheels, cylinders and motion, and the rearward one was a six-wheeled 'truck' under the tender. This arrangement involved the use of flexible steam and exhaust pipes. Because of this articulation the locomotive could operate satisfactorily on a 14-degree curve. Like the Festiniog 'double-engines', most of the Mason–Fairlie locomotives were built for railways having narrow-gauge tracks; but the Mexican 2–6–6 illustrated, of which 15 were built in 1890 by the Baldwin Locomotive Company, were for standard gauge. They had cylinders 20 in. by 24 in., coupled wheels 4 ft. 1 in. diameter and a boiler pressure of 130 lb. per sq. in. The grate area, for burning low grade fuel, was large, 29·8 sq. ft., and the total weight of the locomotive in working was 77¼ tons.

89 Imperial Royal Austrian State Railways: Composite First- and Second-Class Corridor Carriage.

Towards the end of the nineteenth century, there were signs of a general improvement in passenger rolling stock on the continent of Europe and this illustration of an Austrian composite is typical of the trend. This carriage included two first-class compartments and one *coupé*, five second-class compartments, seating eight passengers in each, and a brakeman's box at one end. Entrance was made only at the ends, and

the end doors were recessed into the vestibules to minimise the width when open. An interesting and curious feature was that the clerestory was not central with the car body but with the compartments so as to give a symmetrical effect when seen from inside. When the windows were lowered there was a rail across the opening about half way up to prevent passengers leaning out. The first-class compartments were upholstered in crimson plush; each contained a folding table attached to the car sides. Lattice sun blinds of wood were fitted to all windows, in addition to the usual spring roller blinds. The lighting was by compressed oil gas.

90 Belfast and Northern Counties Railway: First-Class Dining Car.

The vogue of the dining car spread rapidly on the railways of the United Kingdom, and as rapidly to Ireland as elsewhere. The Belfast and Northern Counties had no runs of any great length, for its main line extended no further than from Belfast to Londonderry; but it served a beautiful district, particularly in the Antrim coast resorts, and towards the end of the nineteenth century strenuous efforts were being made to develop the tourist traffic. The very handsome, and ornately furnished, dining car was put on to the crack trains between Belfast and Portrush. Actually the length of the run, from end to end, was just long enough to serve a single sitting of lunch or dinner, and the car had no corridor connection with the rest of the train. Very luxurious seating accommodation was provided for no more than 24 passengers, and it is a fair indication of the habits of the day that only 6 of these seats were in a smoking compartment. The car was built in the Belfast shops of the company, and it was notable in being electrically lighted in the later 1890s.

91 Imperial Government Railway of Japan: Third-Class Bogie Carriage.

This illustration shows a type of carriage built in England by the Metropolitan Railway Carriage and Wagon Co., about 1892–3. The seating plan was quite open inside except for two lavatory cubicles in the centre. On each side of this central portion, where the light shows through in the picture, there were four back-to-back seats accommodating a total of 24 passengers in each group; but on the opposite side of the carriage, immediately beneath the windows, was a long, continuous bench. Thus many of the passengers sat either facing or with their backs to the engine as in ordinary European compartment stock, while others sat sideways as in many an old-fashioned English tram. The roof was of the 'concealed Clerestory' type as in the four-wheeled carriage, ref. 21. Carriages built by British manufacturers were almost invariably of teak, with the natural wood varnished. When indigenous manufacture began, it was no more than natural to use native-grown timber; but the grain of that used was not so pleasing as that of teak, and so they were usually painted black or brown.

92 Midland Railway of England: A Twelve-Wheeled Composite Carriage of 1879.

The Midland Railway was in the forefront of British railway carriage development in the nineteenth century, and the opening of the Settle and Carlisle line in 1876 and the inauguration of new Anglo-Scottish services, required the finest possible rolling stock. The new services both to Glasgow, in partnership with the Glasgow and South Western, and to Edinburgh jointly with the North British, were highly competitive. Thomas Clayton produced some beautiful carriages for the new trains, and the illustration shows a 12-wheeled composite of 1879. They were lettered 'M.S.J.S.'—Midland Scottish Joint Stock—but at a later date distinction was made between those going different ways north of the Border. The lettering then became 'M. & G.S.W.' or 'M. & N.B.' as the case might be. These Midland 'composites' included only first- and third-class accommodation, for the Midland had abolished the second class on all the trains as from 1 January 1875. These Midland twelve-wheelers were non-corridor, and they did not last long after corridor trains became general. They were too long to be used on branch lines and secondary trains. In their 'day', which lasted for more than 20 years, they were second to none.

93 Chicago, Burlington and Quincy Railroad: A High-Speed 'Columbia' Type 2–4–2 of 1895.

With the introduction of the Wootten type of firebox spreading out to a greater width than the diameter of the boiler, locomotive designers sought wheel arrangements other than the popular 'American', in order to accommodate these large fireboxes in rear of the driving wheels. The first engine of the 2–4–2 type in the U.S.A. was built by the Baldwin Locomotive Company in 1893, and exhibited at the World's Fair in Chicago in that year. It was named *Columbia*, and the type took its name from that locomotive. There were, of course, by that time many engines of the same wheel arrangement in Europe. Two years later, however, the Chicago, Burlington and Quincy Railroad took delivery of the remarkable engine illustrated. It had cylinders 19 in. diameter by 26 in. stroke; coupled wheels of no less than 7 ft. diameter, and carried a boiler pressure of 200 lb. per sq. in. It was designed for high speed, and it did not disappoint its designer or owners. But it proved an unsteady rider, and was subsequently rebuilt as a 4–4–2. The 2–4–2 type was short-lived in the U.S.A. The 4–4–2 gave the same facilities for accommodating a large fire-box at the rear end, while the leading bogie gave greater stability in high-speed running.

94 Midland Railway, England: A Johnson 'Spinner' 4–2–2 of 1896.

In 1887, great interest was caused in the British locomotive world by a revival in building of 'single driver' locomotives for express passenger work on the Midland Railway. Previous to that none but coupled engines—2–4–0 or 4–4–0—had been built for passenger working on the Midland for the past 21 years. The revival was partly due to the invention of the steam sanding gear, which was such a help in preventing wheel-slip when a locomotive was starting away with a heavy train. But they were locomotives of advanced design for their day, and being very economical on coal, were great favourites with the drivers and firemen. Sixty of these engines were built between 1887 and 1893, some with 7 ft. 4 in. and some with 7 ft. 6 in. driving wheels, and with 18 in. or 18½ in. cylinders. Ten of a still larger variety were built at Derby in 1895, but the finest group of all were the '115' class

illustrated, of 1896, which had driving wheels 7 ft. 9 in. diameter, and cylinders as large as 19½ in. diameter, by 26 in. stroke. The boiler pressure was 170 lb. per sq. in. Besides being magnificent engines to look upon they were superb runners. Engine No. 117 of this class shares with a North Eastern 4–2–2 the record for the highest fully authenticated speed attained by a British locomotive in the nineteenth century, namely 90 m.p.h. They could tackle heavy trains too, as well as run extremely fast, and a record exists of No. 125 taking a train of no less than 325 tons from Kettering to Nottingham 51¾ miles in 59 minutes. Engine No. 118 of this class is preserved in the railway museum at Leicester.

95 Paris–Orleans Railway: A 2–4–0 Locomotive for Light Trains.

This curious little engine, which was one of a class of nine originally put into service in 1856–7 on the one-time 'Grand Central' railway of France, provides an interesting contrast to the general run of nineteenth century French locomotives. The great majority of these, both for passenger and goods service had either outside cylinders or outside frames—or both. One thinks in terms of the influence left by such men as Crampton and Buddicom. But this design, with inside cylinders and inside frames throughout, looks French only in respect of the colossal steam dome, the 'dustbin' type of sandbox on top of the boiler, and the array of pipes festooned on the outside. The Orleans railway found plenty of use for these little engines, and from 1889 onwards put on improved boilers. They were, however, definitely designed for light trains, and cannot have had much of a turn of speed. The cylinders were 15 in. diameter by 22 in. stroke, had coupled wheels 5 ft. 5 in. diameter, while the boilers had 1,042 sq. ft. of heating surface and a grate area of only 10·8 sq. ft. The weight of the engine only was 30 tons in working order.

96 Eastern Railway of France: A Famous 2–4–0 Locomotive of 1878.

In the previous volume of this series, *The Dawn of World Railways 1800–1850*, various examples of the celebrated Crampton type of locomotive, a kind of railway 'stern-wheeler', were illustrated; and in *Railways at the Turn of the Century 1895–1905*, there was illustrated the famous survivor, *Le Continent*, which is happily preserved. The Crampton type proved so popular on the Eastern Railway of France that when more powerful locomotives were required, a 'Crampton' with four-coupled wheels was designed, and eleven engines of the remarkable design illustrated were put into service in 1878. When the 'Orient Express' was introduced in 1883, engines of this class were used to haul it on the first stage of the run eastwards from Paris. These engines were noteworthy for having coupled wheels of no less than 7 ft. 7 in. diameter, and were run regularly at speeds up to 75 m.p.h. They proved so successful that two further varieties were put to work. One class, for general express passenger service, had coupled wheels of 6 ft. 11 in. diameter—again very large—and the second, for mixed traffic, 6 ft. 0 in. diameter. Over 60 engines of this 'four-coupled Crampton' type were built. The 'super' flyers, used on the Orient Express, had cylinders $17\frac{3}{4}$ in. diameter by $25\frac{1}{4}$ in. stroke, and carried a boiler pressure of 143 lb. per sq. in. For 2–4–0s they were heavy engines, and in

working order weighed 45 tons without their tenders.

97 The First British Sleeping Car: North British Railway, 1873

Although sleeping accommodation in varying degrees of comfort had been provided on North American railways for some years nothing special had been considered necessary for the relatively short runs in Great Britain. After all, the rigours of an all-night journey by stage coach were still within living memories in the 1860s. The first British sleeper was, rather surprisingly, built by the North British Railway, not by one of the wealthier English companies engaged in the Anglo-Scottish business, and it was run between Glasgow and King's Cross on the East Coast route via Edinburgh and York. There were two three-berth sleeping compartments, with the berths arranged longitudinally, so that the passengers lay three abreast. There was a compartment for luggage at one end, and an ordinary second-class 'sitting-up' compartment at the other. This was provided for the convenience of first-class sleeping passengers who wished to have their personal servants close at hand. The use of longitudinal berths was adopted in various other early British designs of sleeping car and followed, in this respect, the early North American Pullman sleepers. The pioneer North British car was completely self-contained, being run some years before the introduction of corridor trains.

98 Eastern Counties Railway, England: A Special Horse Box.

The 'Eastern Counties' was the largest constituent of the Great Eastern Railway, and although it later became involved in a most intense suburban business in East London, it was primarily a line of the East Anglian shires, and had a large agricultural traffic. Among other railways, it had the nickname 'Sweedy'. The conveyance of horses was an important item. Passengers might be herded together in open trucks, but where animals of any kind were concerned, the inherent English love of animals, and abhorrence of any form of cruelty to them, led to the design of many interesting railway vehicles. This smart little van was designed so that both sides opened completely; the lower portion, hinged horizontally at the bottom, folded down to make a broad platform to bridge any gap between loading dock and vehicle floor, while the upper portion opened upwards. A further interesting provision was the inclusion of dog 'boots' on either side of the central horse compartment. These were divided on the centre line of the vehicle, thus providing accommodation for eight dogs, each in a separate 'Kennel'.

99 Toledo, St. Louis and Kansas City Railroad: A 'Business Car'.

An interesting feature of the North American railway scene which developed in the nineteenth century and is still continued today, is the 'business car'. This is a private saloon used by railway officials when on tour, or is available for hiring to companies or individuals when travelling. They are provided with day and night accommodation; private cooking facilities and ample scope for entertainment of guests, while the day saloon usually takes the form of a parlour, or conference room, where business can be transacted. Today one frequently sees one or more business cars attached to the rear of long-distance express trains. The design of the car illustrated is in marked contrast to the British six-wheeled, first-class sleeping car, and is clearly intended to run on the characteristic sharply curved and lightly laid tracks of the 1860s and 1870s in the U.S.A. The car itself is quite traditional in its body design, with entrances only at the ends, and a high clerestory roof. Like many American cars of this period, the exterior finish was merely that of the natural varnished wood.

100 The Pullman Car in England: A Midland Railway Drawing-room Car.

The Midland Railway was the first British line to use the Pullman form of car, in 1874. They were purchased from the U.S.A., shipped in parts and erected at Derby. They differed from the normal American type in having the larger carriage wheels customary in England, and the difference in this respect can be very clearly seen by comparison of this car with that under reference 99. The Midland cars were originally 'sleepers' put on to the night Scottish services; but the one illustrated was later converted into a very ornate drawing-room car. This Midland enterprise was regarded with the greatest disfavour on some other railways, where the use of such large vehicles was thought to constitute a definite danger. It was not so much the big cars themselves, but their use in trains of mixed stock. It was feared that in a collision, one such car would crush to pieces all the smaller four- and six-wheeled vehicles in a train. Happily, such forebodings proved to be largely ill-founded, and the Midland Pullmans can be said to have started the trend towards longer and more luxurious carriages in England.

101 **Great Northern Railway, England:** Sturrock's Masterpiece, the '264' class.

The aspirations of Archibald Sturrock, in building ever larger and more powerful locomotives, reached its climax in 1866 with the production of six 2–4–0 locomotives that were huge for the period, with 7 ft. diameter coupled wheels, 17 in. by 24 in. cylinders, a very large boiler and still larger firebox. Strangely enough, however, their influence on the railway of their origin was practically *nil*. Mr. Sturrock retired not long after they had taken the road, and his successor, Patrick Stirling, did not believe in coupled engines for express passenger traffic. He took an early opportunity to rebuild them as 2–2–2 'singles' with his own design of 'straight-back' boiler. The original engines, as 2–4–0s, were massively built, with outside frames, and the unusual provision of additional stays between the horn guides of the leading coupled wheels, and those of the leading carrying wheels. They were intended to work hard, and those frames were designed to absorb heavy stresses. But although they did not fit in with Patrick Stirling's ideas these engines created an immense impression in France, as described under reference 102.

102 **Northern Railway of France:** The 'Outrance' 4–4–0.

With the development of its traffic in the 1860s, the Northern Railway of France made a study of various English express locomotive designs, and decided to base the future practice on Sturrock's '264' class (ref. 101). The first examples, with the usual unsightly French boiler mountings of the day, were built as 2–4–0s, but the long rigid wheelbase did not take kindly to the somewhat indifferent French permanent way, and in 1877 a 4–4–0 version was produced, including a leading bogie. The massive double-framed construction for the coupled wheels was retained, and the engines were a great success. They were used, as Sturrock intended his Great Northern 2–4–0s to be used, *hard*! The frames stood up to heavy driving, and they became nicknamed the 'Outrance' engines—the 'all-out' engines. There were 50 of them in service on the Nord; the cylinder dimensions were the same as the G.N.R. 2–4–0s, 17 in. by 24 in., and the coupled wheels 7 ft. diameter. The fact that these dimensions were retained for locomotives that were standard in France until the 1890s is an indication of how far in advance of his time Sturrock was.

103 **London and North Western Railway:** A Webb Three-Cylinder Compound of 1885.

In developing the compound system of propulsion, F. W. Webb adopted a curious form of mechanical design, in that he used two high-pressure cylinders, exhausting into a single low-pressure cylinder. A more logical arrangement would appear to have been to have one high-pressure and two low-pressure, to retain roughly equal volumes of cylinders and sizes of working parts. As it was, the high-pressure cylinders had to be made very small, and the one low-pressure cylinder, the front of which is prominent in the illustration, was huge. It also gave the singular accoustic effect of only half the normal number of exhaust beats. But there was another curious feature about all Webb's three-cylinder compound passenger engines: the two pairs of driving wheels were not coupled. The high-pressure cylinders drove on to the rear pair, while the low-pressure drove on to the leading pair. The engine was thus something of a 'double-single', which was hoped to have the freedom of a 'single-wheeler' with the power of a coupled engine. On the L.N.W.R., however, other factors combined to prevent that happy state of affairs from materialising, and the engines illustrated were not very speedy.

104 **Northern Railway of France:** The First Four-Cylinder Compound Engine.

This engine, No. 701, seems to have been directly inspired by Webb's work on the L.N.W.R. in England. It was originally built as a 2-2-2 in 1885, but the collaboration between Alfred de Glehn of the Société Alsacienne, in Belfort, and M. du Bousquet, the locomotive engineer of the Nord, resulted in the use of two low-pressure cylinders instead of one—a much better balanced arrangement. But like Webb, the French engineers did not couple the two pairs of driving wheels. The division of the drive between two axles appealed to du Bousquet, because the heavy use of the 'Outrance' 4-4-0s was leading occasionally to broken driving axles. Engine No. 701 was not entirely a success as a 2-2-2, and in 1892 she was rebuilt in the form illustrated, and became, in effect, a compound version of the 'Outrance'. As a compound she was very successful, and became the forerunner of a lengthy series of four-cylinder compounds on the Nord. In all subsequent engines, however, the two pairs of driving wheels were coupled. Engine No. 701 has been preserved, and is now in the French railway museum at Mulhouse.

105 **Belgian State Railways:** The 'Columbia', or Type 12, 2-4-2 Express Locomotive.

So far as British practice was concerned the 2-4-2 type for tender engines was practically unknown, though at one time it was quite popular on the continent of Europe. It was, of course, a natural development from the 2-4-0 for railways requiring to use a larger firebox than could be accommodated between a rear pair of driving wheels. The Belgian 'Columbia' class, introduced in 1888, was a very striking example of this wheel arrangement, in its use of inside cylinders, very deep and massive outside plate frames and a notably long boiler. But to British eyes the most arresting feature was the *square* funnel! This was standard in Belgium until 1896, and was abandoned only on a new series of these 2-4-2 express locomotives built in the following year. Some of the earliest engines of this class had six-wheeled tenders; but in later batches a four-wheeled design was used with a carrying capacity of coal and water almost equal to the six-wheeled type, and much lighter. The cylinders were 19·8 in. diameter by 23·6 in. stroke, and the coupled wheels 6 ft. 10½ in. diameter. No fewer than 114 were built of the type illustrated, and many more, with circular chimneys, were added from 1897 onwards.

106 **Paris, Lyons and Mediterranean Railway:** The First 2-4-2 Express Locomotives.

While the Belgian locomotive illustrated under reference 105 represents one of the last examples of the 2-4-2 tender engine for express work, the P.L.M. engine of 1868 was one of the earliest. This company had for many years used the Crampton type, but locomotives with only a single pair of driving wheels soon proved inadequate for the heavy work on this line, particularly for the section through the Cote d'Or mountains north of Dijon. The new 2-4-2s were introduced in 1868, batches built simultaneously at the company's works in Paris, and at Oullins, near Lyons. They were originally built as 2-4-0s, but they developed a pitching action at speed and the rear axle was subsequently added. As such they proved very successful. A total of 50 was built, followed by 60 of larger proportions, from 1876. The 2-4-2 type was finally confirmed as the standard express passenger engine of the P.L.M. in 1879 when Monsieur Henry brought out the largest version, of which no fewer than 290 were built, between that date and 1883. It is of interest to recall that a batch of 40 of these latter engines was constructed by Messrs. Sharp, Stewart & Co. of Manchester. The original 2-4-2s, as illustrated, had 16·7 in. by 25·8 in. cylinders, 6 ft. 7 in. coupled wheels and a boiler pressure of 115 lb. per sq. in.

107 **Northern Railway of France:** De Glehn Four-Cylinder Compound 4-4-0.

In the illustrations references 103–106, the development that led up to the earliest four-cylinder compounds on the Nord is depicted. The embodiment of the Webb principle of having two uncoupled driving axles on the French locomotive No. 701 is referred to. While Webb persisted in this practice for his later three-cylinder compound express locomotives on the London and North Western Railway it was not continued in France after the first experimental locomotive. The Webb compounds in England would have been much better had the axles been coupled. What might

be termed the first 'production-batch' of de Glehn four-cylinder compounds on the Nord is shown in this illustration. It had a boiler not much larger than the original 'Outrance' class, but proved very successful, and provided the forerunner of two further classes of 4-4-0 compound, before M. du Bousquet, in collaboration with Mr. A. de Glehn, produced the famous Nord 'Atlantics'. The engine illustrated was one of a class of 17 dating from 1891, and carrying what was then the high boiler pressure of 199 lb. per sq. in.

108 **The St. Gotthard Railway:** Four-cylinder Compound 4-6-0 Locomotive.

One of the first railways outside France to adopt the de Glehn arrangement of compounding, with two high-pressure cylinders outside, and two low-pressure inside, was the St. Gotthard Railway in Switzerland. Mention has already been made in this book (ref. 74) to the exceptional gradients leading to the great tunnel under the Alps, and locomotives of exceptional power and efficiency were obviously called for. The de Glehn compound system, though primarily intended for high-speed passenger work proved itself admirably suited to hard 'slogging' service on mountain gradients, and the locomotives illustrated, forming a class of 17, and put into service from 1894 onwards, were very successful. Although designed and built in Switzerland at the works of the Swiss Locomotive Works at Winterthur, they have a distinct 'French' look about them. They had the de Glehn feature of a 'starting valve' that enabled live steam to be admitted to all four cylinders—a most useful provision on such a line. The cylinder diameters were $14\frac{5}{8}$ in. high pressure, $23\frac{1}{4}$ in. low pressure, with a common stroke of $23\frac{5}{8}$ in.; the coupled wheel diameter was 5 ft. 3 in. and the boiler pressure 225 lb. per sq. in.

109 Canadian Pacific Railway: The First Locomotive built by the Company.

Although the great trans-continental line was not completed until 1885, there was considerable activity east of the Rocky Mountains before that time, and a works of considerable size and capacity had been set up on De Lorimier Avenue in Montreal. It was here that the first locomotive to be built by the Canadian Pacific Railway was completed in 1883. Its designer, F. R. F. Brown, was a Scotsman of wide experience; he trained in Great Britain and worked on the Great Indian Peninsula and the Grand Trunk Railway before joining the C.P.R. As will be seen from the illustration, engine No. 285 was a typical 'American' type 4–4–0, though having very neat lines. While in England the 4–4–0 was essentially a passenger type, in North America, during the 'eighties' of last century, it was a general service class, and throughout this period about 90 per cent of all C.P.R. locomotives were of this wheel arrangement. Engine No. 285 put in 37 years of hard work before being scrapped in 1920. She had 17 in. by 24 in. cylinders; 5 ft. 2 in. coupled wheels, and carried a boiler pressure of 150 lb. per sq. in.

110 Canadian Pacific Railway: Stoney Creek Viaduct in the Selkirk Mountains.

In its dramatic passage from the prairie lands of Alberta to Pacific tidewater near Vancouver, the C.P.R. had to cut through two tremendous mountain barriers. First there was the main range of the Rockies, and then the almost equally fearsome Selkirks. Had the engineers been willing to accept a very long detour, the crossing

of the Selkirks could have been avoided by following what is known as the Big Bend of the Columbia River; but this would have added no less than fifty miles to the journey. After suffering incredible hardships in a primeval mountain wilderness, the surveyors found a pass through the Selkirks, even though it involved gradients of 1 in 45; and it was near the summit of the line, at Glacier, British Columbia, that Stoney Creek had to be crossed. The illustration shows the original timber trestle viaduct across this ravine. It has now been replaced by a steel-arch girder bridge. The line makes a spectacular S-bend in the approach to this viaduct from the west and today it is a favourite spot for the official photographers of C.P. Rail to pose special passenger and freight trains in dramatic scenery.

111 Canadian   Pacific   Railway: Entrance Porch to the Earliest Type of First-Class Sleeping Car.

The great size and stately proportions of this carriage serve to emphasise the great difference between North American and British night travel in the last two decades of the nineteenth century. One has only to compare it with the first British sleeper car (ref. 97). In Canada the contrast was heightened by the use of great bogie vehicles of this type, carried on six-wheeled bogies, yet hauled by relatively small 4–4–0 locomotives, which had not the power of contemporary British 2–4–0s, let alone such powerful engines as the Adams 4–4–0s on the London and South Western Railway. It is true that 4–4–0s like the '285', ref. 109, were not used as train engines in the mountains; but as previously mentioned they were almost universal elsewhere. The coach builder's art was lavished upon first-class cars in Canada.

One notes particularly the beautiful wrought iron work on the balconies, and the fine panelling of the bodies. In the early days of the C.P.R. the finish, like that of the majority of North American carriages, was plain varnish over natural wood; in later years, however, the colour became Tuscan red.

112 London, Brighton and South Coast Railway: The 'Gladstone' Class 0–4–2.

William Stroudley, locomotive engineer of the L.B. & S.C.R. from 1870 until his death in 1889, was one of the greatest individualists in steam locomotive history. He stood for nothing less than perfection in both workmanship and external finish, and one always feels that the apparent anachronism of having gaily painted, *yellow* engines working in some of the dirtiest and smokiest districts of South London was that the yellow livery *would* show the dirt, and compel the cleaning that he always insisted upon. The 'Gladstone' class of express passenger engines, of which 36 were eventually built, provided the 'neon-lights' display of the Brighton motive power stud. The first of them was completed in 1882, and 26 of them had been completed by the time of Stroudley's death. Another ten were built in 1890–1. They were as successful as they were beautiful, hauling heavy trains with notable economy in fuel. The outstanding feature of their design was to have the coupled wheels in front, which Stroudley considered gave smoother riding. They had 18¼ in. by 26 in. cylinders; 6 ft. 6 in. coupled wheels, and a boiler that was relatively large for the period and carrying a pressure of 150 lb. per sq. in. The majority of these splendid engines had a life of about 40 years.

113 Great Eastern Railway, England: The Holden 'T19' Class of 2–4–0 Express Locomotive.

While Stroudley was unique among locomotive engineers in using the 0–4–2 type for his principal express passenger locomotives, those engineers who continued to use six-wheeled engines generally preferred the 2–4–0. On the Great Eastern, however, James Holden built otherwise identical locomotives of the 2–4–0 and 2–2–2 type. Both had the same boiler; both had 18 in. by 24 in. cylinders, and driving wheels 7 ft. diameter. Of these the 2–4–0 was the standard, to such an extent that no fewer than 110 were built, and they were in use all over the system. The 2–2–2 version of the same design was introduced in 1889, three years after the first of the 2–4–0s took the road. Only 20 of the 'singles' were built; but although they did good work they had a relatively short life. Great Eastern engines of that period were called upon to pull heavy trains, but they rarely got the chance to perform any sustained fast running, and in those circumstances the 2–4–0s were undoubtedly the better investment. A number of engines of both the 2–2–2 and 2–4–0 varieties, as well as many other Great Eastern locomotives, were equipped for oil-burning, not because there was then any shortage of coal, but because the Great Eastern had on hand considerable quantities of tar as a waste product from its oil-gas works at Stratford. The illustration shows one of the 2–4–0s equipped for oil-firing.

114 Great Western Railway, England: A 2–2–2 Express Locomotive of the 'Sir Alexander' Class.

In the latter part of the nineteenth century, Great Western motive power had many different aspects. The through expresses from London to the West of England were still operated on the broad gauge (7 ft.), while Wolverhampton works was a stronghold of the standard gauge stud. At the same time, locomotive superintendents had to plan ahead for when complete conversion of the gauge took place, and gradually build up a stock of locomotives that could take over—overnight as it were —the duties formerly undertaken by the famous Gooch 4-2-2s. Hence there was considerable activity in modernising locomotives originally built solely for narrow-gauge duties, and an interesting example is shown in this illustration. The 'Sir Alexander' class of 2-2-2 had originally been built at Swindon in 1875 with 'straightback' domeless boilers. They had 18 in. by 24 in. cylinders, and driving wheels 7 ft. in diameter. Engine No. 1126, as illustrated, was rebuilt at Wolverhampton, with a raised firebox, a new domed boiler and, as if to mark the change more directly, it received the Wolverhampton type chimney, which had a cast-iron top, without the characteristic copper adornment of Swindon.

115 **London and South Western Railway:** An 'Adams' 6 ft. 7 in. Express Locomotive, Class 'T 3'.

The 4-4-0 express locomotives built by William Adams at Nine Elms works in 1883-95 were among the most outstanding, certainly in contemporary British practice, and perhaps even of the entire railway world. As outside-cylinder 4-4-0s, they could claim some affinity to the typical 'American' type of the period; but there was all the difference in the world when it came to external appearances. They had a high thermal efficiency, and indeed their performance was very fully documented in papers read before some of the learned institutions. But the main point for emphasis is that whereas some of his contemporaries sought to obtain higher efficiency by compounding, or the use of special 'gadgets', Adams achieved as good, or better, results with extreme simplicity in design, sound engineering principles and superb workmanship in construction. There were two main varieties of these engines, 30 of each—a 6 ft. 7 in. class as illustrated, and a similar one with 7 ft. 1 in. coupled wheels. Both had 19 in. by 26 in. cylinders, and both were equally successful. They were fast runners, frequently exceeding 75 m.p.h.; one of these engines has been preserved in the Museum of Transport, Clapham.

116 **Victorian Railways:** The 'B' Class 2-4-0 of 1862.

These beautiful little engines were of the type often described as 'Old English', with outside frames throughout, inside cylinders, and the picturesque outside coupling rods. The original orders were divided between Beyer, Peacock & Co., and R. & W. Hawthorn—a total of 26 engines—and they were put into service between 1862 and 1864. As originally built they had spark-arresting chimneys, but in later years their appearance was greatly improved by having the standard cast-iron type. They were certainly among the most ornate of Australian locomotives, with a wealth of brass and copper work, but being very strongly built in the best traditions of the British locomotive industry of the period, they were long-lived, despite the hard work they were constantly asked to perform. Although they were displaced from the more important duties after the introduction of the 4–4–0 type they were frequently called upon to assist with heavy trains, and it was not unusual to see a 4–4–0 and a 2–4–0 together on inter-State expresses about the turn of the century. The 'B' class 2–4–0s were on first-class express duty for more than 20 years.

117 **Victorian Railways:** A First-Class 'Sitting' Carriage of 1883.

All the early passenger rolling stock for the Victorian Railways was imported from England, and although much of it at first reflected the rather spartan conditions of travel on the home railways the actual construction was first class, with the bodies built in ash, American oak or teak, with mahogany panels. As in the New South Wales coach (ref. 79) they had double roofs as a means of insulation against the heat of the sun during the brief, but very hot, Victorian summer. In time American influences began to come in, and the carriage illustrated, which dates from 1883, shows an unmistakable likeness to American bogie vehicles, in its high clerestory roof, and its bar-framed bogies. Early Australian bogie vehicles always seemed to have a rather spidery appearance below the body, and the bogie wheelbase was in any case very short. The car illustrated was designed for 'domestic' service within the State of Victoria, and prior to the inauguration of the inter-State services there were no unduly long journeys radiating from Melbourne. This particular example is designated a 'sitting' carriage, indicating that no provision was made for passengers to lie down full length. Internally it was of the usual American type, with entrances at the ends.

118 **Victorian Railways:** The 'Old A' Class 4–4–0 of 1884.

In 1882, the New South Wales railways had felt the need for a passenger locomotive that could run freely at higher speeds than the celebrated '79' class (ref. 30), and Beyer, Peacock's had built the first of a series of inside-cylinder 4–4–0s of strikingly British appearance, with inside cylinders, inside frames throughout and the Bissell truck 'bogie', as on the '79' class. They had 17 in. by 26 in. cylinders, 6 ft. diameter coupled wheels and a boiler pressure of 150 lb. per sq. in. Because of their speediness they became known as the 'Peacock Highflyers'. Their fame spread southwards, so much so that the Victorian Railways ordered 10 of them adapted for the 5 ft. 3 in. gauge, and these engines, also built by Beyer, Peacock's took the road in 1884. The main line of the Victorian Railways between Melbourne and the State boundary at Albury is very suitable for fast running, and the 'Old A' class, as they became known, were ideal for the job. The design was developed into the 'New A' class, of generally larger proportions, of which the 15 engines were built at the Phoenix Foundry, Ballarat. One of these latter is illustrated in a companion volume, *Railways at the Turn of the Century 1895–1905*.

119 **Victorian Railways:** A Mann Boudoir Car.

The completion of the 5 ft. 3 in.-gauge line through from Melbourne to Adelaide in 1887, over the tracks of the Victorian and South Australian Railways, clearly called for passenger rolling stock of an improved kind. The new through service between the Capital Cities, opened on 19 January 1887, was the first to be run in

Australia on which passengers could travel between two State capitals without changing carriages, and for over 40 years it remained the *only* instance, due to the diversity of rail gauges in the various states. The beautiful Mann Boudoir Cars, imported from America specially for the new inter-State expresses, were the first sleeping cars to be run in Victoria. Although they were wood-panelled, and incorporated most of the traditional styles in coach construction, they were immediately recognisable externally by their high elliptical roofs—as distinct from the typical American clerestory. At the time they were considered to be the last word in both comfort and elegance, and they continued on the Melbourne–Adelaide service for many years. The bogies, which were six-wheeled, had plate, instead of bar, frames and looked much more solid in consequence.

120 Imperial Government Railways of Japan: A 4–4–0 used on the Emperor's Train.

Prior to the year 1906 there were a number of different railways in Japan, of which the Imperial Government system was only one. Then came a general amalgamation to form the Japanese National Railways. The former I.G.R. is interesting, as its main line was the original Tokaido line, the name of which has recently become world famous in railway circles as that of the entirely new super-speed main line on which speeds of 150 m.p.h. are reached. Practically all the equipment for the original line came from Great Britain, and the handsome 4–4–0 illustrated was purchased from Kitson's of Leeds in 1873 as an 0–6–0. It must provide one of the rare examples of a goods engine being converted to passenger

work. This rebuilding was done in the Kobe shops in 1876. It made an extremely neat little engine, and one that was in high favour. The photograph from which this illustration was made shows the engine highly decorated for working the Emperor's train at Kyoto. That the appearance is wholly British goes almost without saying; there is not even a cow-catcher, or heavy canopied cab, to take away the impression.

121 Imperial Government Railways of Japan: 4–4–0 Express Passenger Engine.

Following the rebuilding of the early Kitson 0–6–0 as a 4–4–0, this type became for a time the standard passenger locomotive on the I.G.R. The main line largely followed the coast southwards from Tokyo, and with the light rolling stock and easy gradients, no very high tractive power was needed. One could scarcely imagine a more English-looking locomotive than No. 44, the subject of our illustration. The only oriental sign is the small louvred shutter in the cab side. But the straight running plate, deep, though slotted, splashers, inside Stephenson link motion and British-type headlamps, all complete the 'home-rails' impression. This engine was one of a small class built by Kitson's of Leeds in 1876. Orders for additional 4–4–0 locomotives went to other British manufacturers, including Neilsons of Glasgow, who put their own features of detail equipment into these early Japanese locomotives (*see also* ref. 134).

122 Hakone Line, Japan: An American-built 2–6–0 of 1897.

In a previous volume of this series dealing with railways at the turn of the century, information was not then available regarding any appropriate Japanese locomotives for inclusion. Now that deficiency has been amply rectified, and in this illustration and in the succeeding one the strict period covered by the present book is slightly overstepped to show the marked change in trend in Japanese motive power practice that was becoming evident at the end of the nineteenth century. Locomotives were needed for the heavily graded Hakone Line, where there is a bank of 1 in 40, and Moguls of the type illustrated were purchased from the Rogers Locomotive Company of Paterson, New Jersey in 1897. It was a typical American job of the period, with outside cylinders, inside Stephenson link motion, working flat side valves through rocking levers. There was a single-bar crosshead guide, and double bogie tender. British influences remained in the orthodox buffer beam and three-link coupling, also the vacuum brake. Other American specialities were the huge cab and sandbox on the boiler top—looking like a second dome. This was altogether a most interesting locomotive of what may be called the transitional stage.

123 **Sanyo Railway, Japan:** An American-built 4–4–0 Express Passenger Engine.

If the Mogul of the Hakone line represents one stage in the Americanising of the Japanese railways this 4–4–0 of 1900, built by Schenectady, carries the transition still further. For here is the traditional 'American' 4–4–0, so familiar on the railways of the U.S.A. and Canada, adapted to Japanese practice—still with the standard British buffers and couplings and an element of 'dolling up' in the copper-capped chimney and polished brass dome

and sandbox, but with the American bar-frames, huge cab, bogie tender and giant headlamp. But the most interesting construction feature is the crosshead and its guide, which is exceptionally narrow. It is interesting to see how the American-built locomotives with bar frames had to include the inclined bar-supports for the English-type buffer-beams. This feature was to be seen in many other Japanese locomotives of the period. It was used on the Great Western Railway of England, by G. J. Churchward, to provide additional support for the buffer beams on locomotives having a leading pony-truck, because on all these locomotives the frames did not run continuously from rear to front, as in the usual plate-frame construction, but had the front portion spliced on.

124 **Bengal Nagpur Railway:** The 'A' Class, Mixed Traffic 4–6–0 of 1888.

In the latter part of the nineteenth century, motive power on the broad-gauge (5 ft. 6 in.) lines in India tended to follow contemporary British practice with 4–4–0s or 2–4–0s for passenger and mail trains, and 0–6–0 for goods. But the increase in weight of trains, and the moderate speeds required at the time, led, not infrequently, to the requisitioning of 0–6–0s for heavy passenger trains. The usefulness of a small-wheeled, six-coupled locomotive led to the development of the mixed-traffic 4–6–0. The North Western had what was known as the 'L' class, some with 4 ft. 2 in. and some with 4 ft. 3 in. coupled wheels, while from 1885 some almost identical engines, also known as Class 'L', were built for H.E.H. the Nizam of Hyderabad's Guaranteed State Railway—to give it its full title. The illustration under this reference shows the similar engines purchased by the Bengal Nagpur in 1888–91. Apart from their cow-catchers, 'sunshade' cabs and the ugly 'dustbin' sandboxes, they were of typically British appearance, with their straight running plates, outside cylinders and inside valve gear and handsomely shaped chimneys and domes. It is shown here in the later style of painting, with the number in large numerals on the tender.

125 New South Wales Government Railway: The '131' Class 2-8-0 Goods Engine of 1879.

Although the British locomotives in ever-extending use in Australia were giving very good service, the tremendously rapid development of the American locomotive industry, and the feeling that railway operating in the U.S.A. was more akin to that of Australia than was the British, led to the trial of certain American-built locomotives in New South Wales. The Baldwin Locomotive Co. supplied some 4-4-0s of the typical 'American' type, for comparison with the Beyer, Peacock '79' class (ref. 30), and this illustration shows a design of 2-8-0 introduced in 1879. These were very powerful engines, having 20 in. by 24 in. cylinders, 4 ft. 1 in. diameter coupled wheels and a boiler pressure of 130 lb. per sq. in. They had 'diamond'-shaped smoke stacks, and ornamental domes and sandboxes, though later engines of the class had the standard Baldwin straight chimney. The cab was typically American, built astride the firebox, and placing the driver high up on the right-hand side. The fireman was low down on the tender, and fed the firehole across the fall-plate between engine and tender. They were fitted later with standard N.S.W.

boilers and mountings, though they retained their huge American cabs. There were 11 in all, and the last of them was scrapped in 1937.

126 New South Wales Government Railways: The '205' Class 2-6-0 of 1881.

That the earliest American locomotives in New South Wales did not make sufficient immediate impression to change policy is shown by the placing of an order for 20 powerful goods engines of the 2-6-0 type with Beyer, Peacock. These engines, of which one of the earliest examples is illustrated, went into service in 1881–2. A further 30 followed in 1883–4, and the final batch of 20—making 70 in all—went into traffic in 1885. They were as typically British as the '131' class was American; very neat and handsomely proportioned, with plate frames and inside Stephenson link motion, while the first two batches had no more than a canopy over the footplate. One feels that a closed-in cab was not required, otherwise the builders would have been instructed to provide it. They created a deep impression in England, where engineers of wide experience considered them to be in advance of contemporary practice on the 'home' railways. They had 18 in. by 26 in. cylinders; 4 ft. diameter coupled wheels and a boiler pressure of 140 lb. per sq. in. They did excellent work, both on main line goods and in rendering rear-end banking assistance. One of these engines has been preserved.

127 Imperial Government Railways of Japan: 4-4-0 Express Passenger Engine.

There are some interesting changes in detail design to be noted in successive batches of British-built locomotives for the Japanese railways. Under references 120 and 121 in this book can be seen two versions of the Kitson style, with straight running plate and horizontal cylinders. In engine No. 44 (ref. 121) the line of the smokebox is curved outwards, to provide an enclosure for steam pipes taken direct from the smokebox itself to the cylinders. In the present subject the locomotive is fitted with an outside bar-framed bogie, and to give clearance for this the cylinders are inclined, and the running plate sloped upwards to remain above the cylinder itself and the slide bars. The crosshead is of the single-bar type underhung from the bar. Despite these changes, the general appearance of the locomotive remained wholly British in character. It will be noticed that a much larger tender is used on this engine to that on the Kitson locomotive, reference 121. The engine number was carried in large brass figures on the smokebox door, and not on the chimney, as in earlier Japanese locomotives. These engines, which were built by Neilson & Co. in Glasgow, were used in hauling express trains on the Tokaido line between Tokyo and Kobe.

128 **Canadian Pacific Railway:** A Colonist Sleeping Car.

In its great national task of assisting in the settlement of Canada, and the developing of its resources, the Canadian Pacific Railway had to be equipped to convey large numbers of newly arrived emigrants from Europe, with their families and belongings, who had very little money and could afford to travel only in the cheapest possible way. A large number of such emigrants were bound for the promising farm lands west of Lake Superior, and long journeys were involved, with periods of night travel. The illustration under this reference gives an excellent impression of the facilities provided in these cars. The seats were plain enough, though comfortably shaped, while from the roof below the clerestory, massive bunks could be let down, on which travellers could prepare improvised beds and lie full length for the long night journeys. Both clerestory and saloon windows could be opened as desired, and ample hooks were provided on which hats, garments and so on could be hung. The lighting was by oil lamps. To those accustomed to night travel in the pokey little third-class carriages of Great Britain, and worse still those of continental Europe, these Canadian colonist cars must have seemed the height of luxury.

129 **Canadian Pacific Railway:** Interior of a First-Class Carriage, 1895.

Sumptuous accommodation was provided for first-class passengers on the Canadian Pacific Railway. On the trans-continental express, there were boudoir and observation cars, in addition to fine sleepers. The observation cars had open platforms at the back, though it was probably only the few railway enthusiasts of the age who would stay out on those open platforms when trains were ascending the tremendous gradients on the Rocky Mountains, and a bank engine would be blasting away 'flat-out' within a few feet of that rear platform! Our picture, however, shows a carriage that does not appear to be convertible for night use, and which would be used on the short runs in the eastern provinces, such as Montreal to Quebec, Montreal to Toronto and so on. The interior decoration is more akin to some stately baronial hall than a railway carriage, with its bannistered fencing, pillared supports and the elegant scroll metal-work in the racks over the windows. The thick carpet, and heavy red flush seats add the finished touches of nineteenth-century opulence in travel to this remarkable interior.

130 New Zealand Government Railways: The 'K' Class 2–4–2 of 1877.

In the mid-seventies the N.Z.G.R. had a locomotive engineer, A. D. Smith by name, who believed that American locomotives were more suited to the conditions of working in New Zealand than anything that could then be obtained from Great Britain. On his recommendation, and strongly against sentiments locally expressed at the time, an order was placed with the Rogers Locomotive Company, of Paterson, New Jersey, for two smart little 2–4–2s; and these proved so successful that another six were ordered, and delivered in 1878. On first arrival they were contemptuously described as Yankee toys; but the enginemen soon found they were capable of hard work, and they became warmly appreciated. They were put on the passenger service between Christchurch and Dunedin, and did very good work. The trains were not heavy; neither were they fast. The run of 230 miles took 11 hours. These essentially 'American' engines had cylinders 12 in. diameter by 20 in. stroke; coupled wheels of 4 ft. 1⅛ in. diameter and carried a boiler pressure of 160 lb. per sq. in. They put in nearly ten years on the most important trains, and very many more on secondary services. The last of them was not scrapped until 1928.

131 New Zealand Government Railways: The 'N' Class 2–6–2 of 1885.

When it became necessary to have more powerful locomotives than the 'K' class

for the South Island passenger service between Christchurch and Dunedin, the administration again turned to the U.S.A. and an order for six 2–6–2s was placed with the Baldwin Locomotive Company. But although these engines had considerably larger cylinders than the 'K' class, the boiler pressure was unusually low for the period, only 135 lb. per sq. in. Nevertheless, because of their larger cylinders, these engines had a 30 per-cent increase in tractive effort over the 'K' class, and with six-coupled wheels and greater adhesion weight, they were more reliable in adverse conditions. They seemed equally at home in passenger and freight service, and were many times authentically recorded at 60 m.p.h. In goods service they hauled trains of 600 to 700 tons at speeds of 20–25 m.p.h. on level track. After 15 years on the principal South Island trains they were transferred to the North Island to work the Wellington–Napier mail trains. These engines, like the 'K' class, were long-lived, and the last of them was not withdrawn until 1934.

132 New Zealand Government Railways: A Freight 'P' Class 2–8–0 of 1887.

A powerful freight engine was needed for slow speed duties at around 20 m.p.h., and 'P' class, consisting of ten locomotives, was built in Manchester by Nasmyth, Wilson & Co. Designed for the 3 ft. 6 in. gauge, they were handsomely proportioned and looked a good deal larger than they actually were. The cylinders in particular had the look of some gigantic American type, but were no more than 15 in. diameter by 20 in. stroke. They were tucked in ahead of the coupled wheels, so much so that the pony truck out in front looked almost like an afterthought. On arrival in New Zealand, seven of them were allocated to the province of Otago, working from Dunedin, while the remaining three went to Auckland. They were fine, strong engines, and hauled loads up to 1,000 tons on the level—a remarkable performance on the 3 ft. 6 in. gauge for a locomotive weighing no more than $32\frac{1}{2}$ tons. They put in many years of hard work. The first was withdrawn in 1922, and the last of them, on the South Island, was not scrapped until 1930. Their coupled wheels were no more than 3 ft. 5 in. diameter, and the boiler pressure 135 lb. per sq. in.

133 New Zealand Government Railways: A 2-6-2 Tank Engine for Steep-Incline Working.

The New Zealand railways constructed to the 3 ft. 6 in. gauge in very hilly country abounds in steep gradients and severe curvature. Special locomotives were needed to provide banking assistance on some of the worst inclines. From the inception of its railways in 1863, the New Zealand administrations had purchased their locomotives from contractors, although gradually setting up fine shops at Addington, Wellington. In 1889, however, the N.Z.G.R. built its first locomotives, and an excellent job they were. These sturdy little 2-6-2 tanks were designed specially for bank engine work on the Upper Hutt incline, where the most severe gradient is 1 in 35. They had cylinders 14 in. diameter by 20 in. stroke; coupled wheels 3 ft. $0\frac{1}{2}$ in. diameter and an all-up weight of 37 tons. They might have been more handsome had it not been traditional in New Zealand to mount the sandboxes on the boiler top. There were two of these erections, looking like a couple of glorified dustbins, albeit well polished! There were

only two of these engines, it is true, but their usefulness was such that both put in some 70 years of service, and the first of the two has been restored to its original livery for permanent exhibition at Addington shops.

134 Philadelphia and Reading Railroad: A 'Vauclain' Compound 2-4-2.

The Philadelphia and Reading was at one time one of the fastest running lines in the U.S.A., and its 'Atlantic City Flyers' were sharply timed. The attraction of the 2-4-2 type ('Columbia') in preference to the 4-4-0 was that it enabled a short, wide firebox to be used, of a type ideal for burning lower grade fuels. But there were two other features that distinguished these 'Reading' express locomotives: the 'Mother Hubbard' cab, half way along the boiler, which gave the driver a better look-out and avoided obscuring the view by steam beating down, and secondly the Vauclain system of compounding. This latter system had the great constructional advantage of having all four cylinders outside, with the high pressure located above its corresponding low pressure, and with both pistons connected to a common crosshead. One had the benefit of a balanced mechanism and a straight driving axle, without any cranks inside. Although a large number of compound locomotives of various types were built for service in the U.S.A. the complications did not prove worth while, despite the slightly higher thermal efficiencies obtained with the best designs.

The 'Columbia' wheel arrangement proved rather unstable on a fast-running locomotive, and was superseded by the 'Atlantic' (4-4-2) which had the stabilising effect of a leading bogie.

143

135 Texas and Pacific Railroad: 0-6-0 Shunting Locomotive.

The position of the shunting locomotive, or 'Switcher', as it is known in North America, has always been greatly different from its counterpart in Great Britain and on the continent of Europe. In America the tank engine has never been popular, and the 'switchers' were more or less invariably short-wheelbase tender engines of the 0-6-0 or 0-8-0 type. The tenders were fairly large too, providing ample fuel supplies for long rosters of duty. All such refinements as leading or trailing 'trucks', to improve the riding, were dispensed with, and the whole weight of the engine made available for adhesion. It was also desirable to make the locomotive readily operable in both directions of running, and the Texas and Pacific engine illustrated has the rear end of the tender sloped down so as to improve the driver's view when running tender first, and backing down to a train. The sanding arrangement also provided for both directions of working, with two sandboxes, each feeding ahead of the driving wheels. The engine, which was built in the company's own shops at Lancaster, had cylinders 17 in. by 24 in.; coupled wheels 4 ft. 4 in. diameter and a boiler pressure of 150 lb. per sq. in.

136 Chicago, Milwaukee and St. Paul: An Early 'Pacific' Locomotive.

It could be thought that the 4-6-2, or 'Pacific' type of locomotive was just as logical a development from the 4-4-2, or 'Atlantic', as the 'Atlantic' itself was from the 'Columbia' or 2-4-2. All three wheel arrangements had the advantage of providing space at the rear end for a large and wide firebox, spreading over the frames, if need be. But there is evidence to suggest

that the 'Pacific' type did not originate that way. A large 4-6-0 for the Chicago, Milwaukee and St. Paul was built by Schenectady in 1889; but it proved too heavy for the track, and in less than a year she was modified by the addition of a pair of small trailing wheels under the cab. It is in this form that she is illustrated. One cannot for certain claim her as the *first ever* 'Pacific'; but she was certainly one of the very first, although becoming so almost by accident. She was the only one of her kind, and in the course of her life was several times renumbered. But the really odd thing is that in 1912 she was converted back to the 4-6-0 type. Altogether she bore five different numbers. The original, as illustrated, was 796; then in succession came 191, 850, 6000 and finally 2185. Not the least unusual point about this locomotive is that she bore successively the numbers of two famous British locomotives, 850 being the Southern *Lord Nelson* and 6000, of course, the *King George V*.

37 Baltimore and Ohio Railroad: 4-6-0 Express Passenger Locomotive.

A natural outcome of the popularity of the 4-4-0 or 'American' type of locomotive in the U.S.A. was its development into the 4-6-0—known as the 'Ten-Wheeler', and this example from the Baltimore and Ohio is typical of the simplest version of the type. It was an express passenger design, with 6 ft. 6 in. coupled wheels, and despite the American desire to have as much as possible outside, the valve gear—in this case Stephenson's link motion—was inside, and actuated the slide valves through rocking levers. The notable height of the American loading gauge, as compared with British standards, made possible a very high cab, with an excellent look-out ahead of the driver, though the fireman worked at a lower level. It was this separation of the driver's and fireman's position that saw nothing illogical in the 'Mother Hubbard' type of cab, in which the driver was half way forward along the boiler. These B. & O. 4-6-0s had cylinders 21 in. diameter by 26 in. stroke, and worked at a pressure of 190 lb. per sq. in. They were built by the Baldwin Locomotive Company in 1896. They had a fine record of high-speed service in the Philadelphia division of the railroad.

138 Mount Washington Cog Railway: The World's First Rack Railway.

Many travellers will be familiar with the modern 'mountain' rack railways in Switzerland and Austria, but earlier than any of these was the rack railway constructed up Mount Washington, New Hampshire, the highest mountain in 'New England', attaining an altitude of 6,293 ft. This remarkable railway, engineered by Sylvester Marsh, dates from 1869, and has as its 'rack' a steel ladder laid between the running rails, engaged by a cogged wheel on the locomotive. It preceded the first use of the well-known Riggenbach system by about two years. The Mount Washington Railway, of which the author has been a fascinated spectator, has a maximum gradient of 1 in 2·7 on the breath-taking Jacob's Ladder viaduct—a timber trestle structure fully in the North American tradition. To cope with such a gradient the first locomotive, *Old Peppersass*, which is now preserved at the Marshfield Base Station, had a vertical boiler; but the present stud of locomotives, of which *Tip Top* is one, have their boilers inclined, as in various Swiss and Austrian rack loco-motives, so as to make them approximately level when climbing the mountain. The railway is 3½ miles long, and apart from brief intermissions, when the U.S.A. was engaged in the two world wars, it has been in continuous operation since 1869.

139 The Rigi Railway, Switzerland: The First Mountain Railway in Europe.

Niklaus Riggenbach, locomotive engineer of the Swiss Central Railway, had, in 1863, taken out a patent for a rack and pinion system of railway propulsion on steep gradients. There was no immediate outcome of this invention, and at first no application of it was made. But when Riggenbach heard of the successful opening of the Mount Washington Railway, and had been to see it in operation, he hastened to build a line of his own. His patent differed from Sylvester Marsh's in that he used a shaped, trapezoidal section of bar in the rack, whereas Marsh had used plain round rods. The outcome of Riggenbach's belated development of his own ideas was the celebrated Rigi Railway, climbing to the summit of the Rigi overlooking the Lake of Lucerne. It was completed in June 1873, and immediately became a major tourist attraction. The first section was indeed opened as early as May 1871. Like the Mount Washington line, the first locomotive of the Rigi had a vertical boiler, as shown in the illustration. One of them is preserved in the Swiss Museum of Transport, at Lucerne.

140 The Pilatus Railway, Switzerland: The Steepest Rack Railway in the World.

If the Mount Washington Cog Railway was the first ever, and the Rigi the first in Europe, the ascent of Mount Pilatus, also overlooking the Lake of Lucerne, involves the steepest climbing. The difference in level between the base and the summit stations is 5,344 ft., and as this had to be achieved in a distance of a little over 2½ miles, the *average* gradient is 1 in 2·6 throughout, with a maximum steepness of 1 in 2. Edouard Locher, the engineer, considered that the Riggenbach rack system was not adequate for such steepness, and he designed a horizontal rack rail, with horizontal pinions on the locomotive engaging with them, with safety arrangements to prevent the rack and pinion getting out of engagement. When the line was first opened, steam locomotives were used, and as neither the vertical boiler of *Old Peppersass* and its counterparts on the Rigi were considered satisfactory, Locher mounted the boiler of his locomotives athwartships as shown in the illustration. Neither this, nor the vertical boiler seem to have given lasting satisfaction, for both were superseded by an inclined-boiler design in later locomotives. Beautiful models of both original locomotives and carriages of the Pilatus Railway, and of the later types of the Rigi Railway, are in the Swiss Museum of Transport at Lucerne.

141 **The Schafberg Railway, Austria:** A Steam-Operated Survival.

The Swiss mountain railways have now been changed to electric traction, although the Mount Washington Cog still remains steam-worked. But there are several highly picturesque steam mountain railways in Austria. One of the most picturesque of these climbs up the Schafberg to an altitude of 5,400 ft. from St. Wolfgang, in the Salzkammergut district, near Salzburg, and overlooks the very beautiful lake of the Wolfgangsee. The locomotives, as can be

seen from the illustration, are of the conventional 'mountain' type with inclined boiler, and having the o-4-2 wheel arrangement; but the rack system is different from any of those previously described under references 138–140. It is, however, one of the widest used of any and was invented by Dr. Roman Abt in 1882. It uses a toothed rack, as in the Riggenbach, but with two toothed rack rails. The teeth of one rack are in line with the indents of the other, and the locomotive pinions thus engage doubly. The Schafberg railway is still steam-operated during the summer months. In the winter much of the track is so exposed as to be completely buried in snow.

142 **New South Wales Government Railways:** The Hawkesbury River Bridge.

Some 20 miles to the north of Sydney is the great and picturesque inlet of the Hawkesbury River. Some means of crossing it had to be devised because it lay athwart the direct line to the rising industrial city of Newcastle, and thereafter to the Queensland border and the capital city of Brisbane. John Whitton, the able engineer-in-chief of the N.S.W.G.R. selected a site for the crossing, and was confident enough to place contracts for the work; but the Government of the day developed 'cold feet' over the entire project, and they appointed a Board of outside advisors to adjudicate upon the various proposals after the construction of the bridge had been thrown open to world competition. Even so, it was agreed that the Government's own engineer, John Whitton was to make the final recommendation. It was a beautiful design, consisting of seven lattice girder spans, but great difficulty was experienced in constructing some of the supporting piers, which had to be sunk well below water level to reach solid rock. The estuary had a great depth of sand, and in some cases the foundations had to be sunk to more than 100 ft. below high-water mark, where there was solid rock, and to more than *double* that depth where there was sand. The bridge was opened for traffic in 1889, and was undoubtedly the greatest railway civil engineering work in Australia. In this difficult location it gave 50 years of heavy, continuous service; but with deterioration it was found necessary to replace it with a similar but stronger bridge opened in 1946.

143 New South Wales Government Railways: Albury Station.

The construction of railways in Australia proceeded in a piecemeal fashion, complicated by the confusion created by the diversity in rail gauges that developed. One need not go into the history of how New South Wales came to have one guage while Victoria and South Australia had another; but as it happened there was a confrontation across the banks of the Murray River, with the 5 ft. 3 in. gauge of Victoria coming up from the south and the 4 ft. 8½ in. gauge of New South Wales arriving from the north. The Victorians were established at Wodonga in 1873, and the N.S.W.G.R. arrived at Albury in 1881. By mutual agreement the Murray River was bridged, and in 1883 connection was duly made in one of the finest pro-

vincial stations in Australia. Behind the splendid outer façade of Albury station was a single platform, eventually extended to a length of 1,500 ft., and on it all through passengers had to change. The New South Wales train stopped at the north end, and then passengers had to transport themselves and their luggage to the 5 ft. 3 in. gauge Victorian train waiting at the south end to take them on to Melbourne. This state of affairs lasted for nearly 80 years, until the Victorian Railways laid a standard-gauge line from Melbourne to Albury, and one could at last travel in a through train between Sydney and Melbourne.

144-6 THE RACERS OF 1895, East Coast

The nights of 21 and 22 August 1895 witnessed the fastest-sustained long-distance running yet performed anywhere in the world, in the concluding stages of the great 'race' from London to Aberdeen. The train leaving King's Cross at 8 p.m. on 21 August covered the 523 miles to Aberdeen in 520 minutes at a record overall average speed of 60·6 m.p.h. The locomotives belonged to three separate companies, two of each class, and their main features and their achievements were as follows:

144 Great Northern Railway: The Stirling Eight-Foot Bogie Single.

These engines ran the racing train as far as York, one engine relieving another at

Engine no.	Route	Distance (miles)	Time (min.)	Average speed (m.p.h.)
668	Kings Cross–Grantham	105·5	101	62·7
775	Grantham–York	82·7	76	65·3

Grantham. They were of a later variety of Stirling's famous design than that under reference 63, having closed in splashers and various other improvements. The performances put up were very good, with a trailing load of 101 tons; the engines weighed 45·1 tons.

145 North Eastern Railway: W. Wordsell's 'M' Class 4–4–0.

This was one of the heaviest and most powerful locomotives in Great Britain at the time, and included many modern features of design. Again the work was done in two stages, but in this case it was not merely one engine relieving another at Newcastle. The express had to reverse direction in the Central station, and the fact that the second engine had to be attached to what up until then had been the rear of the train, allowed a very smart station stop to be made. The load continued to be 101 tons, and the 'M' class engines weighed 50·7 tons without their tenders.

Engine no.	Route	Distance (miles)	Time (min.)	Average speed (m.p.h.)
1621	York–Newcastle	80·6	79	61·2
1620	Newcastle–Edinburgh	124·4	113	66·1

146 North British Railway: M. Holmes', 6 ft. 6 in. 4–4–0.

In setting down details of the running over the North British line, the exceptionally curving nature of the route must be emphasised. There were very few sections where a driver could settle down to a spell of continuous fast running; speed had to be restrained round many sharp curves, and the intermediate gradients were steep, if not very long. North of Arbroath there was the additional hindrance of single-line working, with slacks for hand exchange of tablets. The North British 4–4–0s employed were of an excellent design and their drivers did wonderful work considering physical hindrances inherent in the route.

The load was reduced to 86 tons north of Edinburgh.

Engine no.	Route	Distance (miles)	Time (min.)	Average speed (m.p.h.)
293	Edinburgh–Dundee	59·2	59	60·2
262	Dundee–Aberdeen	71·0	78	54·7

147–149 THE RACERS OF 1895, West Coast

On the final night of the race the West Coast train leaving Euston at 8 p.m. (22 August) was cut to a load of no more than 72 tons—three bogie coaches—and made the unprecedented time of 512 minutes over the 540 miles to Aberdeen. This, so far as can be traced, is still the fastest time *ever* made between London and Aberdeen by rail. Two railway companies were involved, the London and North Western, as far as Carlisle, and thenceforward the Caledonian. Each used two locomotives, and with only three intermediate stops the length of non-stop run was longer than the East Coast route. The engines concerned, and their performances were as follows:

147 London and North Western Railway: F. W. Webb's Three-Cylinder Compound 'Teutonic' Class.

This was a larger and very much faster development of the type of engine illustrated under reference 103. The engine concerned was the *Adriatic*, No. 1309: Euston–Crewe, 158·1 miles, 148 min., speed 64·1 m.p.h. At Crewe engines were changed, and in place there was attached:

148 London and North Western Railway: 2–4–0 'Precedent' Class No. 790, *Hardwicke*.

She made the following outstanding run

from Crewe to Carlisle: 141 miles, 126 min., 67·2 m.p.h. Inevitably one makes comparison between the performances of the rival engines, and in this the relative weights of the engines must be borne in mind. The L.N.W.R. 'Precedent' was the lightest of any engine engaged in the Race, and weighed no more than 32·7 tons without tender against the 50·7 tons of the North Eastern 'M' class.

From Carlisle northwards the Caledonian Railway used 4–4–0 locomotives representing successive varieties of the same general design. Between Carlisle and Perth the engine was a Drummond 6 ft. 6 in. class, as shown in the illustration (ref. 149).

149 Caledonian Railway: a 'Drummond' 6ft. 6in. 4–4–0.

Between Perth and Aberdeen the engine was the Lambie development, which differed externally only in having closed-in safety valves over the firebox and a plain dome cover. The engine making the run from Carlisle to Perth was handicapped

Engine no.	Route	Distance (miles)	Time (min.)	Average speed (m.p.h.)
90	Carlisle–Perth	150·8	149½	60·4
17	Perth–Aberdeen	89·7	80½	66·8

Railway	Engine class	Weight of engine (tons)	Total load* in relation to engine weight
G.N.R.	'Stirling' 8-footer	45·1	2·98
N.E.R.	'M' class	50·7	2·8
N.B.R.	'Holmes' 4–4–0	40·2	2·95
L.N.W.R.	Webb Compound	45·5	2·18
L.N.W.R.	'Precedent' 2–4–0	32·7	2·98
Caledonian	'Drummond' 4–4–0	45·0	2·48

* Including weight of engine's tender.

on so long a non-stop run because there were no water troughs to replenish the tender *en route*. The overall time might have been considerably faster had the driver not had to ease down towards the end to avoid running out of water.

To assist in a comparison of engine performance the relation of engine weight to train weight is given, in each case counting the weight of the engine's tender as part of the train.

150 New York Central Railroad: 4–4–0 Locomotive No. 999.

Towards the end of the nineteenth century, speeds were increasing rapidly and a number of claims for very high maxima were made on certain railroads in the U.S.A. In England train running had come under the scrutiny of a number of erudite observers, and no claim for a higher maximum speed than 90 m.p.h. was made (see ref. 94). In the year 1893, some very fast running was being made by the Empire State Express, of the New York Central Railroad. Special engines were allocated to the run between New York and Buffalo, of which the 4–4–0 No. 999 was one. So selective was the locomotive allocation that the name of the train was carried on the engine's tender. Two particular runs have been widely quoted, though the actual method of recording has not been subjected to the closest scrutiny. On 9 May 1893, it was claimed that a mile west of Grimesville was covered in 35 seconds, an average speed of 102·8 m.p.h. Two days later the same driver and engine are reputed to have covered the same stretch at an average speed of 112·5 m.p.h. Although these speeds are not nowadays accepted as

fully authenticated, it can be asserted that speeds of around 100 m.p.h. were being attained on this particular run. It is perhaps not without significance that no claims for still higher speeds were made afterwards, even after the fine British running in the Race to the North in 1895.

151 Caledonian Railway: The Second 'Dunalastair' Class 4–4–0.

One could scarcely conclude this account of the formative years of the railways of the world better than with a description of this splendid design of locomotive. It was, in effect, an outcome of the Race to the North in 1895. Mr. J. F. McIntosh's first 'Dunalastair' class, of 1896, was designed to supersede the Drummond 4–4–0s (ref. 149), and they succeeded in proving that they could equal the racing times, but with *double* the loads of 1895. The second 'Dunalastair' class went one better; for after racing stopped, in 1896, the main problem became that of hauling the increasingly luxurious carriages without any reduction in speed, or a recourse to double heading. These engines had cylinders 19 in. diameter by 26 in. stroke, 6 ft. 6 in. coupled wheels and carried a boiler pressure of 175 lb. per sq. in. Only two of them were named; the first engine of this class *Dunalastair 2nd*, and the engine illustrated, the *Bredalbane*. These engines created a most favourable impression in the railway world, and in a companion volume in this series, *Railways at the Turn of the Century 1895–1905*, the story is told of how the design was adopted as a standard by the Belgian National Railways.

BIBLIOGRAPHY

BOOKS

Abdill, George B., *Rails West*, Superior Publishing Co., U.S.A., 1965.

Australian Railway Historical Society, *A Century Plus of Locomotives*: 1855–1965.

Bruce, A. W., *The Steam Locomotive in America*, George Allen & Unwin Ltd., London, 1953.

Harrigan, Leo J., *Victorian Railways to '62*, Victorian Railways Publicity Department, Melbourne, Australia.

Palmer, A. N. and Stewart, W. W., *Cavalcade of New Zealand Locomotives*, Angus and Robertson, London, 1956.

Warren, J. G. H., *A Century of Locomotive Building*, The Locomotive Publishing Co. Ltd., London, 1923.

Weil, P., *Les Chemins de Fer*, Larousse, Paris, 1964.

White, John H. jun., *American Locomotives*, The Johns Hopkins Press, Baltimore, 1968.

PERIODICALS

The Railway Magazine, I.P.C. Business Press Ltd.

The Railway Engineer, I.P.C. Business Press Ltd.

The Locomotive Magazine, Locomotive Publishing Co. Ltd.

Baldwin Locomotives, Journal of the Baldwin Locomotive Co.

INDEX